Bitcoin

A Complete Beginners Guide to Bitcoin Mining, Trading, Blockchains, And the Future

Crypto Tech Academy

The contents of this book may not be reproduced, duplicated or transmitted without direct written permission from the author.

Under no circumstances will any legal responsibility or blame be held against the publisher for any reparation, damages, or monetary loss due to the information herein, either directly or indirectly.

Legal Notice:

This book is copyright protected. This is only for personal use. You cannot amend, distribute, sell, use, quote or paraphrase any part or the content within this book without the consent of the author.

Disclaimer Notice:

Please note the information contained within this document is for educational and entertainment purposes only. Every attempt has been made to provide accurate, up to date and reliable complete information. No warranties of any kind are expressed or implied. Readers acknowledge that the author is not engaging in the rendering of legal, financial, medical or professional advice. The content of this book has been derived from various sources. Please consult a licensed professional before attempting any techniques outlined in this book.

By reading this document, the reader agrees that under no circumstances are is the author responsible for any losses, direct or indirect, which are incurred as a result of the use of information contained within this document, including, but not limited to, —errors, omissions, or inaccuracies.

© Copyright 2018 Dibbly Publishing.

All rights reserved.

Contents

CHAPTER 1 UNDERSTANDING CRYPTOGRAPHY IN BITCOIN _____ 3
    CRYPTOGRAPHY _____ 7
    THE COIN _____ 8
    THE VALUE OF A COIN _____ 15
    BITCOIN ADDRESS _____ 18
    PRIVATE KEYS _____ 19
    PUBLIC KEYS _____ 21
    HACKING BITCOIN _____ 22

CHAPTER 2 ELEMENTS OF THE BLOCKCHAIN _____ 24
    NODES _____ 25
    LEDGER _____ 26
    DOUBLE SPENDING _____ 30
    BLOCKS AND BLOCKCHAINS _____ 32

CHAPTER 3 BITCOIN MINING _____ 34
    HASH FUNCTIONS _____ 35
    PROOF OF WORK _____ 38
    NONCE _____ 40
    MINING RIGS _____ 41

CHAPTER 4 BITCOIN TRADING _____ 42
    MARKET SPECIFICS _____ 43
    MIND FRAME _____ 48
    INSTRUMENTS AVAILABLE _____ 55
    BID-ASK _____ 59

Market Orders	65
Brokers	67
Online Trading	68
Tools and Programs	69
Scanning Tools	71
Exchanges	74
Trading Strategies	88
Retracements	94
Moving Average	97
Exponential Moving Average	98
Average True Range	99
ADX Indicator	117
Trading Gaps at the Open	121
CHAPTER 5 FUTURE OF BITCOIN	**125**
CONCLUSION	**127**
THANK YOU!	**131**

Dibbly Publishing

Dibbly Publishing publishes books that inspire, motivate, and teach readers. Through lessons and knowledge.

Our Book Catalog

Visit https://dibblypublishing.com for our full catalog, new releases, and promotions.

Follow Us on Social Media

Facebook - @dibblypublishing

Twitter - @DibblyPublish

Download Your Bonus:

Bitcoin Profit Secrets

Discover the methods and techniques used by the most successful Bitcoin investors so you too can profit and succeed!

https://dibblypublishing.com/bitcoin-profit-secrets

Preface

The gold standard in the world of cryptocurrencies is a title that belongs to the first cryptocurrency ever to be created and widely accepted – Bitcoin. It came into public view in 2008 and ever since then it has become part of the Internet landscape, especially as the possible alternative to using fiat currencies in an ever-increasingly online world.

This book is designed to appeal to those of you who have never heard of Bitcoin, cryptocurrencies, or blockchains. But it also serves as a valuable resource for those of you who have heard of it but do not fully understand how or why it works. And once you understand, how you can go about using it as a tool in transactions or as an asset to be bought and sold for capital appreciation.

Regardless of your intentions, even if you don't believe in the legitimacy of cryptocurrencies, you should still make the effort to understand their concept, specifically Bitcoin.

Why?

Because cryptocurrencies are here to stay. Unless, of course, the intent itself is wiped away and ecommerce is no longer something the world engages in. Which doesn't seem to be the case at this point — in fact, it looks more realistic that ecommerce is growing in leaps and bounds and we need better ways to transact across borders, ways that are less expensive and more convenient. Fiat currencies do not lend themselves to cross-border commerce, especially in small amounts that online shoppers are used to.

Over the course of this book, what you will find is that the use of cryptography to design the coins or the currency, makes it a foolproof way to obviate the potential of forgery or theft. You will find that it becomes harder for politicians to use currency as a political tool, and that the new economy — which is largely electronic in nature — is better suited to cryptocurrencies. And this book is going to show you how that happens. Basically, the purpose here is not to just introduce you to all the elements involved in Bitcoin, but also to demystify the scary-sounding terms and concepts. By the time you reach the end of this book, you will be an old hand at Bitcoin and its ecosystem.

Chapter 1

Understanding Cryptography in Bitcoin

When you think about a currency, you think about something that is easily exchangeable and can hold the value that you need it to. Let's think about currencies for a second – in their most basic form and why we need them.

The reasons currencies exist is to be able to facilitate income and spending. If you work for a computer company, you can't really be paid in computers – that would be too problematic. You would not be able to take the product that is used as your wage to the grocery store and exchange it for food, or send it to your landlord as rent.

So instead we use something that can be transported easily and be held and exchanged without worry about its value altering while we hold it. These are inflationary effects that modern economics is concerned with. If you earned a dollar today and that dollar was able to buy you a sack of potatoes now, but would only be able to buy you half a sack in a month, then the value of your currency — and by extension the value of your work — has been deemed lesser in value.

What you provide in terms of products and service to your employer or customer, needs to be paid for in a neutral token. Something that can be used in any situation across any platform.

In the last century, currency economics has greatly evolved and matured to the point that we no longer need to barter, or use gold as the medium of exchange. We have now got to the point that we can use a physical token to represent the value that we have earned. We call that currency. But to be clear, nationalistic views aside, that dollar bill we have in our money clip is not what is valued, it merely represents the value.

We have security features in those pieces of paper so that those who are not authorized to print It, can't. As a society we elect a government to take care of things like that and we empower them to take care of it on our behalf. That's a key understanding that you must keep with you throughout the discussion and journey in understanding Bitcoin or any other cryptocurrency for that matter. We give our government the authority to do that so that they can manage the process of the currency and make it easy for us to use and to keep it safe from fraud and manipulation. The reason we need them to do all that is because paper currencies are inherently unsafe. They can be forged; they can be manipulated or stolen – and I am talking about the physical store of value, that dollar bill you have in your money clip.

As we evolved, commercially, we found that it was no longer efficient to just use paper fiats and wire transfers to conduct business. Because we are adopting new methods of commerce. It is trivial to say that online, ecommerce has changed our definition and needs of a token currency. In the past we needed something light to carry (instead of lugging around heavy coins of gold or copper) to exchange with merchants and vendors in the market square. Today we also need that currency to be used in online transactions. We can't seem to be able to tear up paper currency and shove them though electronic cables to be sent to the vendor we are dealing with, so we instead use banks and payment processors and credit cards to effect the payment.

To make a simple payment it involves so many intermediaries and so many wheels to turn just to effect something as simple as a dollar. The reason this is the case, is that the payment we need to send to that person needs to go from our credit card company to a payment processor who then deals with the banking system and then sends your payment across. There are just too many intermediaries involved and that is because this legacy system cannot handle today's online commerce.

It would be like saying we do not want to use planes to fly from San Francisco to London because we want to continue using a horse and carriage.

The horse and carriage constituted the bulk of our transportation technology a century ago and it worked well then because we didn't travel very far, and didn't do it very often. It is also all we knew how to build. This is the same way that fiat currencies (our country's paper and metal coin currencies) relate to commerce. The fiats worked well a generation ago because we bought locally, even if the item was imported. Because storeowners would buy from stockists, stockists would buy from wholesalers, wholesalers would purchase from importers, then importers would deal with foreign exporters. These importers would make large purchases using their banking facilities. But all these middlemen caused the cost of things to inflate. At that time, it was a necessary cost of doing business. Not anymore. I was at an online store the other day and bought everything from moisturizing lotion to art supplies and shoes, and it was significantly cheaper because there was no need to account for costs and mark-ups of all the intermediaries the conventional supply chain presented.

I can even go directly to the seller in a cross-border transaction and buy what I want. None of the purchases I made, and I am sure you can relate to this, needed hard fiat currency. If you think about it, you will realize that this mode of payment is inefficient, ineffective, expensive and outdated.

There is one other thing. Fiat currencies leave room for

fraud and theft in ways that require a special infrastructure to enforce laws and deterrents against bad actors. Bitcoin changes the entire supply chain structure with the ability to allow payments to be processed anywhere in the world – even on Mars – when we get there, with inexpensive and impenetrable means.

As soon as we figured out how to make trains and build ships, we were able to cross the Atlantic by ship and take trains across great lands. Then the plane arrived, and we no longer needed to take two different modes of transport. We just got on a plane in London, and hours later we would arrive in San Francisco. The efficiency of the new mode catapulted the speed of business and the overall wealth of the civilizations we are a part of.

Bitcoin is poised to do the same, because it is more adept at online transactions. Bitcoin can transact within ten minutes and have the payment in the seller's hands at a speed that is unprecedented.

Cryptography

What is cryptography? In its basic form, cryptography is about changing content to something that is unrecognizable to those who are not authorized to consume it. So for instance, the Department of Defense could send its nuclear submarine captain orders, and anyone who intercepts the message could not decipher it because they don't have the proper codes to do so. That's just one example. There are two basic kinds of cryptography. One is where you can process a cipher in one direction, then process it back in the reverse to make it so only the person who is the intended recipient is able to decipher the message.

The Coin

There is no physical coin. This is typically the hardest part for anyone to understand. The vernacular used in cryptocurrencies tries very hard to approximate the language used in ways we can relate to, and that's about as far as it goes. For instance, mining is not really using a pickax to remove bits of currency out of rock, and coin is not bits of round metal that you make from the thing that you mine. These are all just terms that are used in the industry and do not mean what the same thing in other industries.

The coin is not really a physical coin. It is not even an intangible coin. The funny thing about this coin is that it exists, but not in any way that you can touch, hold or observe it. The only reason it exists is because the universe of nodes within the network that you are in says it exists. The bottom line is that you own the coin because the community says you do, and they coin exists because the community says it does.

Let's take this one step further. The community has no choice but to say that a coin exists. They do not have a choice in this matter. The moment it comes into being, the community cannot say that it does not exist – it is not an opinion, it is a fact. It does this through an algorithm that is called the consensus algorithm. In the consensus algorithm, as you will see later, the coin that exists is the one that has a history behind it, and the community backs up its existence.

For all those of you who think that there is a specific coin, albeit one that is cryptographic, I am sorry to say this is the prevailing misunderstanding of Bitcoins. There is no physical product or electronic product – there is only the spirit of the product that exists because the community has agreed that it does. This makes Bitcoin the perfect holder of value. It cannot be created and it cannot be destroyed – it can be sequestered though, and never used again. But human self-interest will protect against that, although human weakness erodes that every time we forget our passwords. When we do, the coins that are stored in that account with a particular private key, are lost to the world of Bitcoin.

Let's start at the beginning of how Bitcoin works and how it comes into being. There are two ways we can answer this question. First, is if we look at the question to refer to the genesis of the crypto currency itself. The second would be to man how each coin comes into being and how it then gets passed from one person to the next. This is the part that is totally interesting and completely novel. It should have been patented but it wasn't, and that is a great way to allow it to flourish.

Bitcoins don't exist and are merely ledger balances which are attributed to the rightful owner by the previous owner and witnessed by the entire community. So, there is no physical manifestation of the coin. Think of it this way. Imagine if every single person in a town of one hundred people used the same bank, and none of those people bought any good or service from beyond that town or the world outside that town. In essence, you would have a closed ecosystem where everyone made and spent their money within the town.

So that town has one bank and all the townspeople have a checking account in that bank. Think about how that would work out. No cash would need to change hands if everyone just used a check to notify the bank to transfer their available balance to the person they identify. So if Alice needed to pay Bob $10, then she would give him a note (we call these checks in today's banking system) that says "Pay Bob $10" and include a signature to indicate to the bank that it was indeed Alice who was giving the instruction. Upon receiving the instruction, the bank would then alter the appropriate ledger balances. It would reduce Alice's balance by $10 and increase Bob's by the same amount. What it would not need to do is actually, or physically, is move a physical $10 bill and give it to Bob. The bank would have a large pile of cash in its vault and the balance that is in each person's account is a testament to how much claim they have to the funds in the vault. You need to picture it in such a way that there is a pool of funds within the vault and the total pool of funds amounts to all the claims that depositors have.

It is the same way with Bitcoin. Contrary to popular belief, coins are never taken out of the system. I've seen some places that tell you that the coin is removed and placed for safe keeping – you can't do that because the coin doesn't really exist. The only thing that you can do is print the string that represents the coin, But even that doesn't do much, because the coin always stays in the system.

Imagine a ledger where all the transactions between members of the community are recorded. Just like the bank in the ongoing example. If you were to go in and remove your Bitcoin from the system, it would be like saying that you could go to the bank and remove a line from the ledger. It can't be done. Even in a bank, it doesn't matter what's taken out of the safe, it's what's in the ledger that matters. If someone empties the contents of the safe, the bank still owes the depositor the value that is stated in the ledger. Because the ledger is the central record of ownership.

In Bitcoin, that ledger keeps all the coins because the coins have no other identity except that of whom the last user and the previous user were — all the way back to the time the coin was created.

When we use physical fiat currencies, the legitimacy of the currency is ascertained by the security features that are embedded in the currency, i.e., serial number, watermarks and so on. We gain assurance from the knowledge that it was printed by a government-sanctioned mint, and issued into circulation by a duly-authorized bank. Plus the fact that there are laws to protect it and agencies to enforce those laws. It is legal tender because the currency is given the force of sovereignty by law.

On the other hand, Bitcoin has none of these, but we take that it is legitimate by at least two systemic features of the coin. The first is that the coin wasn't randomly created – this is most important. Because if anyone could create coins at any point they wished, there would be no ability to create or transmit value, since there would be an oversupply of phony money.

Bitcoin is not phony money because you have to actually work to get it. You can't just buy it from somewhere and inject it into the system. It either already exists in the system, in which case you can buy it from someone who owns an existing coin, or you earn it by doing a service to the Bitcoin community, called mining. More on mining later.

Since Bitcoin can't be produced out of thin air, it passes muster as a realistic and serious tool born out of equitable standards – something from something, not something from nothing. By that I mean, you can't just make it because you feel like it. Currency must be a carrier of value and if it ever this world not carrying any value, it will not be able to carry value as part of its existence in this world. So to make the first coin, there needs to be a reward for that work – and that's where mining comes in. You do some work; you get a coin. Then from there you pass it on to someone else for whatever you want for it in return.

All coins originate in this way and the algorithm that controls bitcoins has a predetermined number of coins that will be released: in total there will be 21 million coins. At the moment, there are just under 17 million coins in circulation with only four million left to be mined into circulation. Once that last coin is mined, there will be a fixed number of coins theoretically available. Theoretically, because the number of coins, while fixed at 21 million, may end up being less because there are coins that fall out of the system constantly. This happens because people sometimes forget their private keys or misplace them, and since they are misplaced, they can never be retrieved. So that means they are lost to the system forever.

Contrary to what most people tend to pontificate, Bitcoin is not designed to take over or replace fiat currencies. It is an integral part of the existing fiat currency ecosystem. In its current state it will not displace the system, and that is a good thing for now.

The entire Bitcoin network really has nothing to do with coins, at least in the way you would imagine. There are no coins at all, actually. They are mere transfers of value and you don't need to represent them with a physical token of some sort. In any transaction, you need three elements: a buyer, a seller and a witness to the ledger entry.

When you have those three things plus the ledger entry, what you experience is a robust system that gives you a credible stream of the transfer of value. Think of it this way: Let's say there is a palette of freshly minted dollar bills. When you work, or trade something of value, the new note is given to you in exchange for the value of your product or service. If it is given to you in exchange for nothing, that currency eventually will end up being worthless – like monopoly money. In essence, for the store of value to be of use, it needs to enter service and to be exchanged for value.

The initial value is that of the mining. As you will see in the next chapter and as it becomes clear to you over the course of this book, mining is a tangible value that is captured and contained within the consideration that is paid for the coin. That initial coin is then paid to the miner who conducts the mining and expends real-world resources. That coin now has tangible value which it is then used by the miner to do one of two things.

He can sell the coin to someone who wants it in return for a different currency – this may include a fiat like the US dollar, British pound or even something more arcane like the Nigerian naira. That exchange between the miner's coin which he received as reward/payment for a service he provided, and the person offering real-world currency, is based on market forces and conditions – just the way the forex market or the stock exchange operates. Buyers and sellers determine the exchange value and it can fluctuate daily, hourly or even moment to moment.

The second thing a miner can do is spend the coin for a product or service. In fact, the first purchase ever made with Bitcoin was from a pizza parlor. Just because Bitcoins can never leave the network does not mean they can't be used to pay for real-world goods.

The Value of a Coin

You may wonder who or what determines the value of a coin. That is a valid question and it deserves a serious look at the economics of exchange and value. This is in essence the fiber of any economic system and that in turn is the fabric of human interaction and commerce. From centuries ago, the first form of commerce was conducted by bartering. The dairy merchant exchanged his milk for the farmer's grain – the farmer got the milk and the butcher got the grain. There was a direct exchange of value fueled by need. It was a better alternative to one person milking his own cow, slaughtering his own meat, farming his own grain, and building his own dwelling. Specialization was indeed a better way of communal living, as long as there was a way to exchange and transmit value.

In the barter system, there was an inherent perception of value. A bottle of milk would be worth a cup of grain, perhaps. But the price was not predictable. What happens when the dairy farmer didn't want grain today? That would deprive the farmer of milk because a barter deal could not be struck. The dairy farmer would have two problems, he couldn't keep the milk till tomorrow at which point he could find another buyer, and he was not able to get the grain he needed to feed himself for that day. To increase the complexity of the transaction, let's say there is a third buyer, who wants the dairyman's milk, but has bricks to sell, and the dairy farmer does not need bricks. That compounds the problem. While barter unlocked the potential of specialization, there was a third element in transactions that could not be solved – and that was the coincidence of need – or to put it in another way, the coinciding of need. If my need for your product does not coincide with your need for mine, it changes the dynamics of the transaction.

To level the playing field, civilization developed currency. Currency held the value of anything. Today it could hold the value of milk; tomorrow it could hold the value of bricks. Currency is not fixed to the tangible product but to the value of the exchange, which can change from one moment to the next even for the same product. With this in mind it is easier to understand why Bitcoins were worth five cents in the early days and then hit a value of $20,000 last year. Human exuberance is not the measure nor value of the cryptocurrency and to confuse the two would be foolish. As a side point, economists are talking about cryptocurrencies and blockchains as a flash in the pan and as having no merit. I agree and disagree with them. I agree with them because the idea that Bitcoin is going to replace fiats is ludicrous. It has neither the infrastructure nor the sovereign backing to do so. But I also disagree, because blockchains and cryptocurrencies are valid mediums of exchange that deconstruct trust and value institutions to the point that a revolution in currency is on the horizon.

In short, currency should be deconstructed into two forms to be able to understand the extent of its use thus far in economics. This also includes its future use, as the nature of society is changed at a fundamental level.

The first is that it is a token to carry the value and to be exchanged for whatever the holder desires. You may use your currency to put food on the table; another may use that money to get medication. Currency has allowed value to be fungible; and cryptocurrency, in turn, has allowed currency to be virtually frictionless. It is indeed the next evolution in value transmission.

The point of all this is that you understand that the physical dollar you have in your hand is different from the value that you need it to represent. In the case of cryptocurrencies, the thing that is being monetized and valued is the expression of transfer. When you look at the details of a blockchain in the following chapters, you should start to realize that instead of a physical coin, or a packet of strings, Bitcoin is merely a message. It is a message that is composed and sent between sender and receiver.

Basically, Bob sends Alice a message saying he has sent her 1 BTC. Alice and the rest of the community are aware of that message. Now because the community knows that Bob sent Alice a message, Alice is the owner of the right to spend 1BTC. When Alice then spends that BTC by buying something from Chuck, she sends a message to Chuck that she is paying him 1BTC, and that message is shared with the whole community. So now the whole community knows that Chuck has access to 1 BTC. Of course, the thing to note here is that we use the names Bob, Alice and Chuck, but in reality, no one knows the identity of the person. They only know the Bitcoin address the message was sent to.

Bitcoin Address

It is the Bitcoin address that has the right to spend that Bitcoin. A typical Bitcoin address is one that begins with the number 1, the number 3, or the string bc1. They are typically 35 characters in length, and are generated in a process that we will explain further on. Addresses starting with the number 1 are older addresses, and those starting with the number 3 or bc1 are newer.

There are three numbers you need to be aware of as far as the Bitcoin protocol is concerned. The first is that it needs a private key, a public key and a Bitcoin address. The Bitcoin address is where a certain value is sent to and it is free to obtain. Each address is unique.

Private Keys

Let's start with the Private Key part of the entire messaging system. The private key is the key (like a password) that you use to access or authenticate the message that you send in a transaction. Remember in a transaction, it is merely a message that you send from one address to another address. In the example above we sent a coin from Bob to Alice. To make sure that Bob's message was authentic, he would have had to sign it with a private key. This private key is unique and it corresponds with the address but you don't get the address first. Instead, the entire process starts with the private key. At its heart, the private key is merely a hash of a random number. And that random number can be any one of 2^{96} numbers That works out to be 8×10^{28}. Just to make a comparison, there are approximately 7.5×10^{18} grains of sand in the whole world. Just keep the quantum of the universe of private keys that are available at the back of your mind.

You can generate a private key for yourself using any means you like as long as the number is between 1 and approximately 2^{96} . There are people who decide to choose private keys that are easily remembered, but this would be a mistake. Because if you can easily remember them, then there is some sort of pattern to them, which in turn means that they are not entirely random. Anything that is not random, can be predicted and brute-forced. So don't do this. You are better off using a truly random generator to get a private key.

There are also ways that you can remember your address and private key and that is by using a brain wallet. In this case you enter a passphrase that only you can know. Take for instance the passphrase "Oh say can you see." This passphrase, when converted using 256-bit SHA results in a private key:

5Htcb6CRnVzqs6nHAWfP79LL1652Pd23oVGmBcRmajdoxVuGPYh.

Once you have this secret key, then the system will generate the corresponding Bitcoin address; in this case the address is 1GQWaMVXm4iZPZvWuXyZRAWKVLCjMPJ8SK.
Just out of curiosity, I did a search at https://blockchain.info/address/ and found that the address is not taken so I could use it if I wanted.

Public Keys

Once you have a private key, the Bitcoin wallet then calculates the corresponding Public Key and the corresponding Bitcoin Address that goes with the private key. So you see the whole thing is actually backwards. You are normally used to creating an email with a user name and then creating the password to go with it. In this case you are actually creating the password first – which is a long, random alphanumeric string, and then deriving the public key from that using the Elliptic Curve Digital Signature Algorithm — ECDSA. You don't need to worry too much about the cryptographic math behind the calculation' except to know that it is a mathematical relationship that is asymmetric. That means you can only go from private key to public key and on to the address; but never from address to public key and back to private key. However, as you will see in the next section, you could try to guess private keys and then find the address from there, but that would be dishonest and almost impossible. That's because it would take you more than the energy of the sun to be able to compute all the existing private key possibilities and the addresses which correspond to that.

Hacking Bitcoin

I wasn't planning to introduce this section into this book, but decided to do it at the last minute just to show you how dangerous it is to use vanity keys or Brain Wallets. You already know that Bitcoin has addresses where coins are stored. It is the only way to have a coin. That address is then 'unlocked' with a private key, which as we said earlier is a random number that you can generate. But now the thing is that many Bitcoin owners decide that they want to have a Vanity Passkey so that it is easy to remember. What they do is use phrases and convert them to keys and addresses. They think — as everyone does — that they can't backtrack from an address to a passkey, but can certainly fall forward from a passkey to an address.

So when you have a phrase that is converted to a passkey, there are bots out there that just continuously check for random phrases and look for addresses that conform to that. When they find it, they just drain the account since they already have the passkey. That's how easy it is to hack a Bitcoin address, especially if the person is not willing to use the protection of random numbers. The moral of the story is that you should always use a random generator for your passkey, and not use a passphrase.

So the lapse in security is not because the system is poor, but because the private key was easily guessed. That is not machine or algorithm error, it's human error.

Chapter 2

Elements of the Blockchain

The Blockchain is the basis of the utility of Bitcoin. Many experts agree that if it weren't for the Blockchain, Bitcoin would have little appeal and value. To really understand the benefits of Bitcoin, you need to understand how the Blockchain works, and by learning this, you can then proceed to understand how the mining process works. Mining is discussed in a later chapter.

The Blockchain is made up of a number of elements that you need to know individually before putting them together and understanding the whole thing. That is how we are going to present the material and you can then build on your understanding, incrementally.

The entre Bitcoin ecosystem is really the Blockchain. That is the genius of the system. As you can see, the coin is a nonexistent imagery – or objectification of a transaction. T's the right conferred on a person to acquire something for something. The value of that something is then transmitted to the next person in return for something of value. We've seen that and we understand that it is just a messaging system that goes from one person to the next and is witnessed by the community.

Underneath the messaging system is a network that is built across a peer-to-peer network. The messaging system would not be of any use if you were to use regular emails.

Why?

Nodes

Because the messaging system needs to be robust and not controllable by any one party, it is spread across a peer-to-peer network. If you used a typical email network as the system, then you leave yourself vulnerable to cracks in the system since it is a server-client relationship across the email network. Instead, Bitcoin uses nodes in a peer network in a distributed system that removes central control, and thereby the possibility of a failure point, from the equation. Each peer in the network is called a node and each node in the Bitcoin network does one of three things. They either originate or receive transactions in the Bitcoin network, verify a transaction, or become miners. We will discuss miners a little later in the chapter again and then look at them thoroughly in a later chapter in the book.

For now, let us look at the a node and understand its

functions, aside from mining. A node is just a computer connected to the internet and has the necessary application to do whatever it needs to do. In this Bitcoin instance, the app is the Bitcoin (that is not a spelling error – the app underlying the node is called Bitcoin) that contains all the software, written in C++. Within each node, it opens up a specific port and disallows anyone from using the node entry to gain access to any parts of the computer. Once the app is established and activated, it turns the computer into a fully functioning node and it can then choose one of two states. The first state is to be a full node and the other is to be a lite node.

A full node is one that downloads the entire ledger, but the lite one only downloads parts of the ledger that pertain to the coins which are relevant to that address.

Ledger

It's time to look at what a ledger is and how it works.

A ledger is a large repository of all the owners of the coins in the Bitcoin system, as well as the trace of transaction that have happened over the course of time from the first day Bitcoin existed. It is worthwhile to remember that there is no actual coin or physical object. There is only a message that transfers value from the Bitcoin system to the miner (which is the first to receive any new coin). When the miner initiates a transaction, he sends a message. The ledger is best visualized as a big book, though it's not. It just keeps a track of how a particular coin has been spent all the way back to its original block.

A typical coin starts its life when it is awarded to the miner. then that transaction is recorded in the ledger and confers the right to the miner to spend x amount of coins. Let's say that is 25 coins (it's not anymore but this is just an example). The ledger then records that message from the system and keeps a note that the miner can spend 25 coins. When he spends 1 BTC, the ledger makes a note of which address that BTC is going to, and now keeps count that this address has 1BTC to spend. If that person decides to spend 0.01 BTC, then the ledger makes note of that and records the address where that 0.01 BTC went.

The ledger is electronic and is stored in full nodes. Partial ledgers are stored in lite nodes. As I said earlier, this partial ledger only stores information of the BTC that it has in its address and where they came from all the way back to the block that it originated from, with the miner that received it. So, let's say you have set up your node to be a lite one and have some coins in it. Then all the transaction history of those coins, all the way back to the coin released by the system and up to the point you own it, will be in the ledger on your node.

The reason full nodes and lite nodes exist is to enable those with limited storage to use Bitcoin and be a part of the network without burdening the system. On the other hand, a full node, while taking up large storage space, is also involved in verifying transactions by looking into its transaction history, i.e., the ledger, and making sure there are enough funds available for the transaction.

Bitcoin is actually facing a bit of a problem these days because most users are not willing to load up on the full node and are only using partial nodes. When it comes to keeping integrity, that can be a real problem and it could end up inadvertently being party to multiple forks down the road. Possibly even a catastrophic double-spending problem — or at worst — outright fraud.

At this point I want it make it absolutely clear that the online world has taken for granted the explanation of the entire Bitcoin structure and existence. People think that a cryptographic coin exists in tangible or electronic terms. It does not. That coin is merely an analogy for the exchange of value. Remember each transaction can be broken down to as small as 0.00000001BTC (1 Satoshi). If a coin existed in physical form, then it would have to be made up of a million tiny coins to make up one coin. The same for its electronic counterpart. This is one way to come to the realization that a full coin in hard or soft terms does not exist. It exists when someone gives it to you. Look at it this way, if I sent you a valid message saying that I am transferring 1BTC to you and you now own 1 BTC, that would show in your account balance, (assuming no transaction fees for this illustration). If you decided to send 100 million addresses 1 Satoshi each, the transactions would go through, but if they were part of a coin, how would you break that up? You couldn't, could you?

That's the point where most attempted explanations on the web break down. There is no physical or intangible coin wrapped in a serial number. It's all just tracks of transactions. It exists only because someone gave it to you, and someone gave it to them, and someone before that gave it and so on… all the way back to the point when the system awarded the miner the bounty for its mining operations.

That's how it works, and all this is kept in the ledger. The ledger is tied up in blocks and the blocks are mined by the miners. Copies of these blocks are kept on every full node. This makes it decentralized and almost indestructible. It also makes it immutable. You can't go back and change a transaction, as you will see in the mining chapter.

Now that you have the ledger and the nodes, let's see how the Blockchain works.

Remember, at the heart of it, the Blockchain is a decentralized messaging system. It obviates the need for trust and it allows all participants to keep track of all the transactions that are initiated in the messages.

As soon as I send Bob a message saying that I am sending him 1BTC, the message is shouted out via a gossip protocol and transmitted to the node next to me. That node I communicate with is a random node that is chosen from anywhere in the world. A handshake from my node to that node takes place and my message is transmitted, in the same way my node transmits that to at least 6 other nodes.

All those are full nodes. My node has a copy of the IPs that are running full nodes. Once I transmit to these six nodes, those ones then verify the transaction. Among other things, the nodes verify that the address which is sending that message has a sufficient balance to make such a payment. They verify that the public key is correct, and a number of other issues too. Once all are good, they pass that transaction on in a gossip protocol where one node tells six or more, and each node after that does the same. There are currently between eight and twelve thousand nodes, depending on the time of day. If each relay jumps to six nodes, then within six jumps ($6^5 = 7776$ and $6^6 = 46656$), that means that the message is broadcast to all the nodes in a fairly short time. But just because they have them doesn't make it safe. There is the danger of double spending.

Double Spending

In a system where you send messages to the recipient, what is stopping anyone from spending each coin more than once? You might think that a boon or a risk, depending on which side of the transaction you are on. The system is a trust-neutral one so it does not leave any of the participants in a situation where they have to trust someone to get a payment. There is no need for that, as long as you get a payment, then it's yours. This is how it works.

As soon as they broadcast a message to you and the nodes verify that there is a sufficient balance, that transaction is placed in a pool for the miners to place in blocks. If the nodes don't verify your transaction for insufficient balances, then you will not be able to spend. But what if what you spent is not yet in a block, and you send out a new message making another payment from the funds you have already sent out?

In many cases that transaction will get sent to the nodes for verification as well. If it is verified and placed in a block, then the second transaction will have a problem because the nodes that are trying to verify your transaction will see that you no longer have the required balance to effect that transaction. So one of the transactions will get rejected. It does not depend on which you made first, it depends on which is placed in the block first. If you make a transaction at T1 and another at T3, if it happens that T3 is placed in a block first, then it is T1 that will not get verified. It will then be rejected. So if you are receiving payment from someone, wait until you get at least two or three confirmations.

Each confirmation you get is an additional block that is going over the one which contains your transaction. The more blocks that go on top of it, shows that the transactions translate to the number of times they are confirmed. It takes an average of ten minutes to create and verify a block. It is fairly certain that after six blocks are created on top, meaning you get six confirmations, and an hour has passed (ten minutes per block x six blocks = one hour and six confirmations), it's a pretty sure bet that your payment is valid and reliable. It doesn't matter where the send is from and where you are located.

Blocks and Blockchains

I am sure you have heard a lot about blocks and blockchains and you would have also probably read a lot about it all across the web. I hate to tell you this, but a lot of the information is wrong. There are some really good sites on the Internet that give you a detailed and esoteric rundown of the Blockchain, but most of the others, as I have mentioned, are far from being remotely accurate.

The Blockchain is the key ingredient in the Bitcoin network. Without the Blockchain, the Bitcoin transaction ledger would be virtually useless. It is the Blockchain that gives the transaction credibility and makes the entire system robust.

What does it do? Or to get a better idea of the entire ecosystem, *how* does it do it?

To put it simply, a blockchain is a string of blocks that make up a chain. Each block is connected inextricably to the block that comes after it, and that block is then linked to the one which comes later. And so as time goes by, each block is tied to the other without the possibility of anyone going back in transaction history and changing the contents of the block.

The way this works is why mining is necessary, and we will discuss that in the mining section.

Chapter 3

Bitcoin Mining

The entire book thus far has been hinging on the eventual understanding of the mining process and how to go about doing it. There are no pickaxes or blasting caps required to remove anything from the ground. Mining is not even the art of finding something physical. Mining is just a word used in the cryptocurrency industry to describe a computational process of calculating hashes of specific elements.

Let me explain.

Each transaction is identified by a transaction ID, and that transaction is placed into a group waiting to be placed in a block. The miner has the prerogative to choose whichever transaction he wants, and most miners choose the transactions that have the highest tips (in addition to the payment fees and senders. So one of the things you can do if you want the fastest block inclusion times, is to bump up the tip, and you will find your transaction gets included very quickly.

There are numerous miners all competing to do something interesting — they pair up all the transaction

IDs and run them through a hash function that returns a single hash. If they have 256 transactions, then they get 128 pairs of transaction IDs. Once each pair is processed, the miners are left with 128 hashes. These are then paired again, and then again until they are left with one final hash. So 256 Transaction IDs become 128 hashes, 128 hashes become 64 hashes, and 64 hashes are paired again and become 32 hashes. That's paired one more time and results in 16, then hashed in pairs again to become 8. The pattern continues down to four, then two, and finally, the last pair is hashed which results in one hash.

Hash Functions

What is a hash?

A hash is a precise, mathematical function that takes the content of a file and condenses it down to a specific set of numbers which is deterministic. Take this random phrase for instance: "apples in the spring" (without the quotations). This particular sentence results in a hash that looks like this:

B5E72AF8031A87A248FC8A6955DF758CFAA97FD9 C0183F38AD6A7ADCB522AF3A

It looks like a random string of alphanumeric characters. And that is what it's supposed to look like. But it is not random. You can try an online convertor for an SHA256 here:

https://passwordsgenerator.net/sha256-hash-generator/

If you took the "apples in the spring" sentence and plugged it in there, you would get the same string of numbers.

The thing about hash functions – and there are many different ones (this one being the 256 SHA, another being the 512 and so on) — is that they are asymmetric. That means you can only go in one direction. If you have the hash, you can't go back to the original text. You also can't reverse engineer it. See how vastly different the hash is after just altering that sentence to this: "Apples in the spring." It is the same sentence except the first letter is capitalized. Now look at the hash and compare it to the earlier one:

6378FFCC7B0529D3E5C5E3885B55805E5167E64A570D6926B491E4D55099CC60

The vast difference in the hash output makes it impossible to reverse engineer the original word, text or phrase. You can even hash an entire book. The point is that if just one alphabet, punctuation, spacing, or an entire chapter is changed, the entire hash that represents it changes drastically.

This is a powerful way to make sure that nothing gets altered once it is recorded. So, take two transaction IDs like these:

97566b492888b59b34a4b88ddd9764c0fef9eb5c6534b69c76e3c9f3f180e2e5

8c11d9ff4f114e0a35e4882cffac1d3476b3e56a752a0c38fccd6d0f4499c0f8

Now, hashing these two transaction IDs, I get:

7595DA286B700671D0256AD0B125EE011A25E12E8CFC9C446EC8090D97D60999

That's the hash for the two transaction IDs. Once I get those hashes and put them in a block, that block becomes part of the history of the Blockchain and those transactions cannot be altered because Bitcoin does not allow you to alter a transaction. If you need to, you have to do a new transaction or ask the person you sent the funds to refund it. There is no reversal in Bitcoin, or Blockchain. Once a transaction is done, there is no way to reverse it because it gets memorialized in the Blockchain.

This is leading up to the actual mining process.

The entire Bitcoin network works because of the algorithm that underlies the system. It is loaded and deployed across each node – and automatically does what it is supposed to do as far as passing on messages of transactions and updating the ledger. Bu the real power comes in the mining process. All miners are also nodes.

This algorithm also does a few other things in terms of monitoring the block creation process. It makes sure that each block is created in a specific amount of time – which is ten minutes. Further, it ensures that the rewards are dished out to the successful miner.

Proof of Work

But to keep within its ten-minute rule, it has to constantly monitor how fast the blocks are being completed and solved. When it finds that the blocks are being solved fast, it increases the difficulty of the output so that the miners have to spend a longer time finding the solution and succeeding at the output, which is called the Proof of Work.

The reason a solution is the proof of work is because you have to do the hash computations to get the solution, and there is no way of guessing it. So if you have found the solution, it is because you worked at it –

that's the proof of your work.

How does this work?

When the miners are creating the block, they have to include the transaction IDs, the header, and everything that is supposed to go into that block — plus one more item called a nonce.

A nonce is a random number, but it's not just any random number. It is the random number that will make the hash of their entire block, including all the transaction IDs, fall within a certain range. It's not as easy as it sounds. Let me show you.

To create the block, you have to take all the transactions that you are including, and also the hash of the previous block and a number of *their* things, including the time stamp and so on. Now when you put those together, you realize that there is nothing you can change in there, so the resulting hash is pretty much fixed. But then you have to add the last item — the nonce – and you can control that nonce. When you change the nonce, the hash for the block changes.

The job of the miner is to put the transactions in the queue into the block, hash it, and then find the nonce which conforms to the format that the Blockchain algorithm specifies.

When there is low hashing power available and the block times increase beyond ten minutes, then the algorithm monitors that situation and reduces the difficulty level so that the miners can get to a solution faster.

Nonce

How do these miners find the solution to the nonce?

They do it at random. The first has the block and includes a random number. If that doesn't give them the desired output, they try it again, and again, and up to millions of times more until they get one of the random number to adjust that has just enough so that the hash falls within the format that the algorithm has assigned.

If you visit https://blockchain.info/charts/hash-rate you will see the total has rate in the entire community that is mining Bitcoin. What does that tell you? Well it tells you how much processing power there is to hash the blocks. The more hashing power there is in the community, the easier it gets to obtain the solution, and when it gets easier, the time to reach the solution decreases. The moment the time decreases, the algorithm raises the difficulty of the target hash and then equalizes the entire community and returns the block rate to ten minutes.

Why does this happen?

This is so that there is a steady and predictable rete of bitcoins entering the market. If you recall, I mentioned that each miner gets a reward for mining. Now you know what mining is – it's just the hashing of the block to get a particular nonce that fits the algorithm's requirements. It's pure processing power that needs to be expended to get the solution. That requires electricity and investment in hardware, and in return for that, miners are given this reward. At this point in time, the reward is 12.5 bitcoins per block. That also means that 12.5 BTC is released into the system every ten minutes. In most cases miners turn around and sell the coins in the market in return for services or dollars, and that creates supply of coins in the system.

Mining Rigs

A rig is a setup that includes the processing The best rig that you can put together would involve one that is built on ASIC technology. ASIC stands for "Application Specific Integrated Circuits." They consume less power and are faster than just running GPUs, and what is more, they are the only technology out there that can compute the hashes fast enough to be able to keep up with the power required today.

The price range varies between five hundred and three thousand dollars per rig, and that does not include the power supplies, the fan or the racks that you need to mount them on.

Chapter 4

Bitcoin Trading

In general, there are four kinds of trading profiles in terms of time with an open position in the market. The four are:

- Position Trading
- Swing Trading
- Day Trading
- Scalping

There are distinct differences between each, and it has to do with the timeframe that the trader holds the position in. In Position trading, there is no end in sight, only a long term goal and the appetite to withhold and adverse price fluctuations.

Position trading is generally performed by fund managers and long-term investors who buy the stock with long-term goals and views. This is not something that you do from a trading perspective when it comes to cryptos, but it may be something you implement when you mine the currency. If you are paying dollars for it, then you are looking to get in and get out.

Swing trading is similar to position trading except it occurs over a shorter time horizon - between days and weeks compared to position trading that can last over years.

Then there is Day trading that does not last for more than a single trading day. Whatever the position and whatever the profitability, the position is also closed out at a certain point in price or a certain point in time before end of market. In Scalping, the time frames are even shorter. Scalping is a subset of day trading in that the positions never last more than a day, and on most occasions, last for mere seconds and minutes, rarely stretching across hours. The strategy here is to take advantage of price discrepancies, spreads, and temporary fluctuations. The defining factor is how long you hold it. The reasons to hold and the strategies employed in holding are discussed in the book, as it unfolds.

Market Specifics

In the US, to be able to day trade regulated equity markets, your brokerage account must have at least $25,000 in equity at all times. There is a widespread belief that day trading has a little more risk to it, and so brokerages and the market in general would prefer that you have a little more staying power just in case there is a temporary fluctuation in price against your position. This is a good thing. It keeps you safe and protects your account in case of loss.

Trading Bitcoin has no such requirements, so you need to be more aware of your circumstances and be clear that the loss could be total. As you set your eyes on the possibility of riches, you should also be as clear about the losses as you can.

To be considered a day trader, there is just one thing that distinguishes you from everyone else — and I am talking about it in terms of how the government defines you. A day trader is anyone, intentionally, or inadvertently, who trades more than four transactions in five days. In crypto markets, you can be trading as much as three or four times in a day.

This is as opposed to what many people think the definition is, when you just repeatedly go in and out of the market on a moment to moment basis. So just keep in mind, the legal definition is a cycle rate that is less than the daily turnover that most people think.

The second thing is that you can be a day trader of almost any commodity that is market traded. This book will focus on one specific market - which are mid to large caps on the main markets. We will not be talking about pink sheets, commodities, futures, or forex. Only cryptocurrencies; specifically Bitcoin.

You can certainly day trade in all of those, but it

unnecessarily ups the risk and puts you further behind the eight ball, so what we have done is looked at the markets that give you the best of returns in the worst of conditions.

As a matter of practice you should also not allocate more than 30% of your total retirement and savings toward day trading activities. That is the max; the actual amount should depend on your situation and you should come up with the total amount based on an in-depth conversation with your financial advisor.

As high as the returns could be, there is a corresponding level of risk. You could not only lose money above and beyond the inflation rate, you could lose the entire value of the account, or even lose more than what you put into it in total.

That's the part that most people do not understand. It is in fact possible to lose $50,000 when you only put in $30,000. So the losses are not limited to what is in the account. Remember that. For this reason you should invest 70% of what you can afford to lose. That way if you wipe yourself out and the loses creep above what's in the account, you have a 30% margin sitting outside that you can use to cover it. It is your buffer.

Once you wipe it all out, you can look at it in one of two ways: you either walk away, or replenish your funds elsewhere and come back in.

What people do not understand, and why others usually

liken this to gambling, is that people who lose tend to double down. Doubling down works when you are playing the odds. When you play the odds, the chance of the second event happening identically to the first are very slim. So when you do play the odds, doubling or tripling down is a fair strategy to make your losses back.

But crypto day trading is not gambling and it is not based on odds or probability. It is based on fundamental factors that are real and human-driven (most of the time). If you threw a pair of dice, you could predict the probability of its combined result. But if you threw the same dice a million times, its pairs would form a pattern. There are real factors causing the market to move in a certain direction and it is not probabilistic, but they are a derivative of probability — that is what technical analysis and charts depict when you study them.

The way to manage day trading is to lay a strong foundation of fundamentals. This refers to the understanding of the numbers, the players, the market, strategy, and more importantly, how the underlying algorithm works — the Blockchain and the wallet.

On top of that, you learn how to apply both statistical (referred to in the industry) and technical analysis.

The next thing is do not be attracted to the wild-west-cowboy nature of the reputation that day traders seem to project. The reality is far from the truth. To really make money at day trading you need to have a disciplined regimen of study. You need to be able to internalize volumes of fundamentals and instinctively understand key technical trading mechanisms. Day trading is about knowledge, attitude, and character. Trust me when I say it is like being a fighter pilot and as much as media likes to paint a picture that fighter pilots are jocks; they aren't. They are well-trained, well-read and stable-minded people.

Because they make sure that all the reports are out on time and that these companies are not even thinking of doing anything but the right thing. As a day trader that is important.

You must have the correct sense of understanding between the mix of fundamental factors and technical factors of the market, and to do that, you need to keep these issues in mind.

As I briefly alluded to above, the fundamental aspect of a stock, as compared to a crypto, is found in research reports, annual reports, press clippings and news. There is only so much you can read and understand but that makes all the difference in the world. Why? Because to understand the fundamentals of the stock gives you an idea of how it works and why it does the what it does. Cryptos on the other hand require that you get an understanding of the temperament and the legal framework of a technology that is still evolving, and evolving slowly. The fundamentals in the crypto world are based on the technical developments, the legal developments and the overall temperature of the industry.

Reading annual reports gives you the in-depth knowledge of the company. SEC regulations and Bourse guidelines give you the comfort that companies and their managers need to give shareholders the full information. Full disclosure is the law of the land and you, as a shareholder or a prospective shareholder, need to make sure that you understand this. But as a crypto investor, you have none of these safeguards.

Mind frame

The mind frame of the day trading discipline is that you take advantage of the market's responses to news and fundamentals as well as the natural tendencies of the market. When you are a long-term investor, you are buying and selling instruments based on their current performance and their potential performance sometime in the future. Day trading functions at a higher level — it is investing in the way the market works and reacts to the stock, its leaders, news, rumors and the overall way the market works. As a day trader you need to know that is how the combination of fundamental analysis and technical analysis works.

Also as a day trader, while you place a lot of trust in your instincts, to say that you should *never* do that would be deluding ourselves. Sure, day traders have ice water flowing through their veins of stainless steel, but instinct isn't always a bad thing. Instinct means that you have internalized the nature of the beast you are up against, and you know how to anticipate its behavior and responses. You know how it is going to react before it reacts, and you are ready for it. That is the holy grail of the day trader.

The instincts are highly useful, especially when you hear the news or the rumor. Or when you hear the issues that are coming out and understand how the asset is going to respond. Remember, there is more than one way to crack an egg. As a day trader you absolutely do not care if it is a bull market or a bear market; you could potentially make money on both markets. The only time you cannot make money is when the market does not move. Or if it moves too slowly or is inconsistent in its speed.

This is the main reason you do not want to day trade pink sheets. They are unpredictable at best, erratic at worst, and the return they offer is not worth the headache and stress that you will undergo to get to the finish line.

There is only one way to make money in pink sheets, and that is to know the whispers of the rumor mill. And since that is illegal, it's not a game you want to play.

Let's come back to technical and fundamental issues of the various markets.

When you understand the fundamental issues which we will cover in the next chapter, you will see that there is a specific way day traders acquire the knowledge they need when compared to the way long-term swing traders acquire theirs. The reason is that if you ended up looking through every nitty-gritty detail of the counter, you are not going to have time to trade. For this reason there is an abridged framework that I will share with you to use as a day trader and get the exact level of knowledge that you need to make your trading more effective.

Once you have an idea of that, you can then look at the measure that I take to skim and understand the news which I divide into micro, industrial and macro. Typically, macro is at the country and systemic level, while micro is at the corporate and individual level. I also add an industry/sector level to my knowledge base when it comes to any sort of trading.

Why?

Because markets move in lockstep to one, two or three of three factors affecting them, and do so at differing levels of impact. Take for instance taxes. Taxes are a macro subject and affect companies at differing levels. If you look at a company that has high sales that are elastic to disposable income then you know that the company is going to have to readjust its projections if the government raises personal taxes. If that happens, the price will fall. Does that matter to you as a day trader? No. It only matters that your bias at the point is that it is going to be a descending market and that you can profit from it by shorting.

That is the overall frame of mind example that you should employ. When you are a day trader there are a number of different ways you can approach the crypto market. You can think of the crypto market in any number of ways including this example:

Try to see the overall cryptocurrency market as varied as the stock exchange, as volatile as the foreign currency exchange and as risky as small cap or pink sheet markets. The various dimensions of the crypto market resemble individual profiles of a different existing market that one may consider for day trading. But the one aspect that slips away from the collective consciousness of the trading community is that crypto currencies bring together something different from all the equity, bond, commodity and forex markets — the fact that you can make your own Bitcoin, or your own Ethereum. Yes, because you can conduct mining operations, you are able to make your own crypto. There are two ways of doing this and I will cover mining and ICO in the later part of the book.

You should not fall in love with counters, industries and positions either. You have to remember that the mindset of a day trader is that he has no attachment to the asset or the position. A day trader is also always looking for reasons to get out of the market, and that reason can be found in one of two ways. He either sees that it has gone against his desired direction, or it has reached the point that it is time to liquidate profitably.

There is no holding and there is no flat tolerance.

Flat tolerance?

You are in the market to make a profit. If you are in a flat market that is neither moving up nor down, and you are tied up in that market waiting for a movement, you are losing opportunity in another counter that is moving (up or down does not matter). Time is indeed money and if you are in the market without any gain, it's time to get out.

While we are on this topic, remember that you should break the market up into four sessions. You should take the Japanese session as well as the London, followed by the East Coast session and ending with the West Coast session. Remember that cryptos are a twenty-four-hour market, traded around the world. So you have to choose two or three of the four markets, and focus on trading those.

Let's come back to flat markets.

In flat markets, where the price moves sideways as a function of time, or where markets do not change in price or relatively slowly as function of time,

Set yourself a metric that is based on an hourly clock and tell yourself that as a day trader you are going to be trading no less than one round trade per session. There are many traders that say that this strategy works against them without giving them the freedom to extend their profits.

One of the things that I personally love about the crypto markets is that they are electronically matched orders. They are not like the open outcry methods of the old stock markets. Open outcry methods are antiquated but still have their purpose in certain bourses. When you are day trading you should trade in the markets that have the most efficient order execution services or electronic price matching. If you rely on a trader to get the asset for you at a certain price, there are times when he doesn't get that price and there are items when he gets the price on its way down rather than on its way up. These kinds of mix-ups and errors will increase your loss rate.

Let me explain briefly how this works in reality.

If you are in an bourse that uses the open outcry market, you can definitely day trade these, except your strategy would be different (this doesn't happen on the crypto markets but you should have a background understanding of it). You may also want to reconsider using a broker to do your day trades in cryptos for you.

When there is a trader getting you the price you asked for, the trader is not so much looking at the timing of the fluctuation, he is looking to fill your order. So let's say you want to enter the market at $1.21 long. You reckon that there is going to be a short play to $1.31 before the market would signal a reversal, and you want to make sure you ride the price on its way up. The time to go from $1.21 to $1.31 is fairly rapid and it is important that you pick up the trade on its way up so that you can liquidate it on its way down. But instead, your trader sees it and gets the order for you long on the return trajectory. That means your entire strategy is busted. On the other hand, if you were in an electronically matched market, you would be able to put the price and grab it on the way up. In crypto day-trading this is very important.

Most of the time those who have experienced the market and gotten out, have done so because they walked into the market with the wrong frame of reference. They walked into the minute-by-minute day trading market with the value trader's long-term mindset.

When you walk in with this kind of mindset you end up seeing only large price moves and large movements, and not the subtle moves and rapid movements. Many people think that they can be both, day traders and value traders. You can't and you shouldn't, because the mindset required to be one or the other are polar opposite in their fundamental nature. Especially when it comes to cryptocurrencies.

Instruments Available

Think of yourself as a general. As a general, you need to pick and choose the arsenal that is available to you and make the best use of it depending on the task at hand. You have to choose the most surgical of all equipment because day trading is a surgical operation requiring a light touch, not a heavy fist.

Cryptos lend themselves very well to online access and day trading. Online accounts are best suited for this. Do not have a broker that you need to call every time you want to make a trade. That will just kill the returns on the day trading effort. Not just because of the extra commissions, but because you will not have granular control of your entry and exit points.

You need a market-specific device; a computer that is set up with redundant online access. Get two different ISPs if you have to, in addition to your wireless broadband on your handheld device if you are trading online. Make sure that you are getting the best feed. I have a T1 line that runs directly to Bloomberg from my Terminal which gives me a highly accurate condition of the market price. This is important if you want to take advantage of the fluctuations, and as a day trader, you do!

The second thing is that you want to make sure you have computers that are dedicated for trading and that they are not used for any other surfing or browsing. You never want to bog your computer down with the threat of viruses. It is a dedicated computer that is meant for trading and should not be multitasked.

The third thing is that you need to have multiple screens and subscriptions to news and data services. If you are not doing any of these, then you are not serious about day trading and you are not going to be successful at it.

The fourth thing is that you have to identify the best assets that move with a certain pattern. Ideally you should be looking at a mix of early cryptos like Bitcoin and more recent ones like Ripple or Ethereum. In my experience, they have provided some of the best returns in day trading.

When you identify the best cryptos for yourself, immediately get yourself on news-based alerts. I do this in two ways. I have a Bloomberg Terminal on my desk and the page is constantly refreshing information on certain events. Then I also have Google Alerts set to the cryptos that I am tracking.

The fifth thing to do is subscribe to analyst's reports of all these cryptos that are in your basket. Choosing the basket is complex and it must be one that is fairly broad, but not so broad that you can't keep up. Remember there are more than 1200 cryptos for you to choose from. Mix it up between cryptos that are volatile and the ones that are stable, always keeping in mind that day trading happens in the midst of volatility.

There is still a lot of homework for you to do and a lot of reading for you to perform. But once you get them, you will understand all the cryptos that are in your repertoire and you will be able to jump on them wherever there is an opportunity.

How do you choose the cryptos to put on the list?

Here are three specific issues that will qualify cryptos for you to look at and then streamline them from there. The first issue that you have to look at is volume.

Why is volume important?

Volume is important because it determines how fast you can get in and how quickly you can get out — liquidity. When it comes to day trading, that is immensely important. It is not so bad if you can't get it; that just means it's a wasted opportunity, which is bad enough. But if you are in and can't get out, then the price is going to whipsaw and you are going to be on the tail end of a loss.

I personally do not look at any crypto that is not doing more 30 million dollars on average. That list reduces the pickings from the over 1200 cryptos out there. There are instances that you can drop below this hard deck, but the extenuating circumstances must be so overwhelming that you move ahead. But those extenuating circumstances are not the norm for me unless there is a new currency that has come online, and it hasn't built up a volume but still draws my interest.

The thing to note is that even if you have only three currencies in your basket, that means you have six counters you can trade. For instance if you have knowledge in Bitcoin, Litecoin and Ethereum, then you will be able to trade USD vs. BTC, vs. LTC, and vs. Ether; that makes three counters. Then there is BTC vs. LTC and BTC vs. Ether. Also there is LTC vs. Ether. So in total you have six possible counters as potential avenues by just looking at three cryptos. If you studied four — let's say you added Bitcoin Cash to the mix — then you have four more avenues making it ten counters, because you have Bitcoin Cash against the dollar, BTC, LTC and Ether. Having ten counters is enough to fill your day and give you sufficient opportunity to enter and exit the market at least four times in a day.

On any given day, these are the approximate volumes of crypto/fiat pairings traded in some of the markets:

USD vs. BTC: approximately half a billion dollars; ETH vs. BTC: approximately a hundred million dollars; ETH vs. USD: approximately seventy-five million dollars, and finally LTC vs. USD: approximately forty million dollars. These volumes

The second thing you need to look at is the volatility.

You can calculate volatility yourself or you can plot the volatility of your counter by choosing it on your Bloomberg terminal.

Why do you want volatility?

Well you don't want just volatility. If volatility is not accompanied by strong volume, then you want to stay away from it. If volatility accompanies volume, then it is a perfect day trader's market. Volatility is not constant. There are days it will be flat and there are days that it will be over the top. You have to find the one that will give you more trading opportunities.

So the first two things are volatility and volume. The ideal pair, and this is hypothetical and rare, is the stock that is constantly swinging up and down in a range and has lots of volume. So you have a buyer and seller every time it traces up and every time it traces back down.

But that's the ideal and you should be waiting for that all the time. The key to day trading is that you are always in and out of the market. For every Bitcoin you have put aside, you should be in and out two trades per session — so that's twice a day. If you are trading on margin, then you should be on 4 stocks per session. (Just remember never go on margin till you know how this game works).

Bid-Ask

One of the telling signs of a stock is its bid-ask spread. This is the spread that you have when you buy or sell the stock. Let's say you looking at a stock that is trading 1236.00. When you go to buy the stock it is going to show 1236.00-70. This means that when you buy, it will cost you 1236.70. If you sold it right back, they will buy it at 1236.00. So, a simultaneous transaction would lose you money. If you bought a round lot (100 shares) this would mean that you would pay $123,670.00, but if you sold it right away you would then sell it for $123,600.00. That's an instant loss of $70, plus brokerage. Bitcoin's spread is anywhere between $70 and $100 on any normal given day. This means that if you walked in right now at $10,000, your buy price would be $11,100 and your selling price would be $11,000. So an instant buy and sell would net you a loss of $100 per Bitcoin plus fees that your broker charges.

When you day trade you want to get used to paying very close attention to these numbers because they can knock you off your profit potential. If you spent the day scalping $50 per trade, you will end up actually losing $50 for every trade if you do not keep an eye on the bid-ask spread.

The strategic thing about bid-ask is that they tell the secret of volatility and what the market makers and brokers really think of the counter. You have to be able to read the tea leaves when it comes to the bid-ask. If you start to see the spread widening, it means that the brokers are starting to see a shift in the balance of supply and demand.

The way many see the bid-ask spread in any asset, whether it is gold, dollar, stock, or even land, is that there is a premium that exists for the intermediary bringing the deal to conclusion. But there is a more important aspect to it. It is reflective of the supply and demand on both sides of the equation. When there is a stable supply and demand, then the spread is purely for the middle man. But when there is a disparity between the supply of buys versus the supply of sells, then you start to see the price pull in that particular direction.

So let's take for instance a situation where the BTC is trading at $10,000. That price is merely relating the last price that was concluded. It does not reflect the price that is going to be struck in the next deal. But it can be an indication of it.

Every facet of a price has its own supply and demand profile. If you see that there are many suppliers trying to get out of the market, what do you think happens? There will be a selling pressure created, and the sellers will start to lower their price. Bids are prices that buyers are willing to pay, while the ask price is what sellers are looking to sell at. And the spread is the relative difference between what buyers want to buy it at, and ask is the price sellers want to sell it at. Obviously how each side values the transaction is different. Buyers want to get the lowest possible price while sellers want to get the highest. That results in a natural spread between the two. However, as the demand side rises and more buyers are looking to buy, the order book (referring to the ledger containing all the incoming orders and instructions) will show a buildup of demand and that will force the sell side to raise its prices. As buying pressure increases, so will prices. So when you see the spread increase, you can automatically read it as an imbalance in buy and sell orders — this is a situation that will result in price movement.

You can also use the spread as a harbinger of what is to come with volume and volatility. When the volume goes up, the spread decreases because the brokers know that they can exit their position easily. When they volatility goes up, the spread moves the other way, going higher. This is the reason you have to calculate your spread for each counter ahead of time so that you know when to break at the top (liquidate a buy position) and when to cut at the bottom (liquidate a short).

In time, you will master the bid-ask and find that it is a powerful intuition to have because it is the most telling tool that most people do not know how to utilize. In cryptos if you see a change in the spread, or more importantly if you observe a change in the trend of the spread, then you should reevaluate your position and reconfirm if the changes in the spread behavior support or diminish your current open position.

There are four items you want to look at when you are watching the spread. The first is the gap and whether it is increasing or decreasing.

That covered, the next thing you want to look at is the last done. This is the price of the stock that was just concluded. As you know, bid and ask prices are a delicate balance of the order book buy-and-sell orders. Remember not all traders are day traders. In fact a large majority of traders are not. So the strategy they employ is different. They place their orders ahead of time and there are orders constantly in the pipeline so market makers and traders typically have an idea of what the orders in the pipeline are.

The way bid-ask is used is to view the trending nature of the spread as well as the last price. If the last price is being settled toward the buyer's bid, it signals a different condition than if the last price is settling towards the seller's asking price. You can see the logic right there. And remember you are not looking for a turn to a bull or bear market - you are looking to see where the orders in the pipeline are going to turn the market — that is what gives the market its short-term price movement. And that is what you want to observe if your intention is to just ride out the current fervor.

The next thing you want to remain observant about is if

the spread starts moving, you know that the market is about to make a move. Specialist traders look at the bid-ask and see that if an otherwise stable bid-ask starts to widen in the direction of the sell, then the market is about to break lower. If the bid-ask starts to widen and the price breaks higher, then get ready to go long. If that is too confusing, just look at it this way. Whenever there is a spread increase, the market is about to reverse and this could be a handy liquidation or entry point for day traders.

If you think about it, you will start to see the logic. There are a couple of ways you can do this effectively. If your quote terminal is powerful, you can track the bid-ask of your favorite pairs and have an alert chime the moment there is a movement in the spread.

The fourth item in the sequence that you should look at is the volume of the orders. Remember we talked about the order book and the bid and ask prices balancing or overwhelming the other? Well, you will be able to see both the bid volume and the ask volume (it depends on the package that you get from your data service).

Value traders do not need this kind of information as much as we day traders and scalpers do. But we are trying to squeeze every penny out of the market and so we have to look at all the cost and profit center is in the system.

Here are a couple of profit center in the arc of a trade.

If you are in a long position, you need to balance your entry price with two difficult variables in the equation. On the one hand you want to get in the trade, on the other hand you want to get the best price possible, and I mean at the granular level, saving the pennies. In day trading you have to take advantage of the moves.

Because there is always going to be a bid and ask price, and those prices are never going to favor you outright, you have to get adept at haggling for them and balance that nature of grabbing every penny with the opportunity cost of not making the trade. This is the first reason that day trading is a skill that is experienced and not just learned from books. The nuance of timing in getting the best price is one that straddles reality and necessity. But this is a good place to start. You will eventually get to feel the buy and sell price and you will be able to make better judgments from there. But for now you need to get a jump on the market.

Once you understand that, the thing you have to remember is to minimize the use of market orders. That is the next topic of discussion in trading BTC or any of the cryptocurrencies.

Market Orders

Never say never. But in this case, when it comes to day

traders and market orders, never put yourself in a position that forces you to enter a market with a market order or exit a market with the same.

Why?

Market orders are specific terms in the trading industry. A little background - When you set yourself up to make a trade (buy or sell), that order goes into a queue - you saw this earlier when we were discussing Bid-Ask spreads. That queue is not necessarily chronological. It is more about price and volume. If something is trading in an open outcry method then that complicates it even more, but if it is electronically traded then the circumstances change as well. This is part of the reason you use online markets to trade. Market makers are managing the trades electronically rather than having traders on the floor trying to secure an order. This makes it much easier to secure a price during day trades. As a day trader, every penny counts, so you need to keep your eye on the ball and stay in control of the transactions. Market orders reduce your control over market entry and exits by relinquishing price selection to the trader or the electronic program that is designed to clear the order books by matching bid and ask.

When you place an order (for illustration purposes let's say it's a buy), that order goes into a queue based on quantity and bid. If you specify the price you want, that is listed on the market maker's screen and he is looking at a list of everyone who wants to buy or sell. He is going to make the trade that is most profitable to him. If you put in a market order that means you no longer control the price that you get or the trade. This is dire in a tight trading band. If you just place a market order that also means that you are rushing for your position - and you never want to do that in day trading - or any trading - but more so in day trading. Remember you are not just up against buyers and sellers and prices, you are also up against time. That means if you lock in a purchase it needs to be tight.

Unless the need to enter the market outweigh the need to have a specific price never enter the market with a Market order. In the event the market shoots, up you could be caught with a position that moves against you in short order.

Brokers

There are a few kinds of brokers that you may have already heard of. There is the full service broker, the discount broker, and then there is the online broker. You want to choose the online broker with the best execution record that you can find - even if the commissions are a little high.

You should be looking for full service brokers who have research but allow you to execute the trade directly without having to do it over the phone . These are a little more expensive but they are worth every penny for the insight that you get from them since these guys have their ears to the ground on most pairs all day every day.

Let me elaborate. You use them for the understanding they have of what the main brokers are doing and you use them so that you get an idea of what the word on the street about the major moves are and what the smart money is expecting.

Alternatively, what you can do is get the research package from some of the information houses. Bloomberg has a ton of research and in many cases included it their terminal packages.

Online Trading

The best way or you to trade is to do it online and do it on systems that are professionally set up. Do not trade on your laptop at the coffee shop. This is serious business, you need to treat it as such. If you are trading at the local Starbucks then you are not where you should be. Here is why.

Latency.

Latency? Latency is the time it takes for your computer

to send data from your computer to the router, from the router to send it to the junction, and for the junction to send it on the back bone and on towards its destination server.

What is displayed on your screen needs to trace the same path, in reverse. In day trading, time is of the essence. If a price happens at T=0 (counted in milliseconds) and it arrives at our screen in let's say 10 milliseconds, you have time to react) but if that same information has to go over an unreliable router at a coffee shop and by the time it gets to you it's 3000 milliseconds - it makes a big difference). I ran down to the Starbucks near my office a little while ago to refill my coffee and to get a test of their ping times and using my laptop I pinged 480 milliseconds. I came back and tried it on my T1 line and got 4 milliseconds.

That's a huge amount of time to be behind when you are in a trade. Coming back to the trading - do it in your office, or your station that is adequate set up. Never try to do this through the web. You will end up only catching the wind once in a while.

The next thing about online trading is that you need to have a dedicated set of terminals for data. I am not trying to sell Bloomberg, but the Bloomberg Terminal is the one that I trust and have used for years. It's expensive but I have more than made up for the investment. Bloomberg has three modes of connection. Two of them run over the internet and one is a private

T1 line that goes straight to Bloomberg's cloud. Choose the last one. The latency is negligible and your trades come out better in the long run.

Tools and Programs

There are four categories of tools that you are going to need. We already looked at one category - which is the terminal and that covers the pricing data stream. But let's look at all the tools that you need to make sense of things and to be able to take advantage of this. I used them in my early days, and still do most of the time. But I have learnt to rely on experience in equal parts as well. However, if you are starter, then you are going to need as much advantage as you can muster because this is serious business. Don't, for one second, think that you can walk to the edge of the plane and jump without the best chute in your sack. Would you skimp on your cams and carabineers when you go rock climbing? No you won't. Same here you need to get the tools that are right for the job and you will see, in the mid- to long-term that the results will speak for themselves and pay for the effort.

There are four sets of tools as follows: News and Alerts, Price Feed, Charts, and Scanning.

We already saw the tools you need to get a good handle

on prices. The other tools and programs you need fall into three distinct baskets. For news and alerts, we touched on it a little earlier. Your Bloomberg Terminal is going to give you a ton of information, and your Google Alerts is going to send you a bunch as well. Next, let's talk about the sophisticated scanning tool you'll need for your arsenal.

Scanning Tools

Scanning is exactly as the name implies. It is a tool that will scout the market and find whatever you specify, and the sophisticated ones do it in real time. So for instance, let's say if you want to find any stock that has an increasing spread (recall that we talked about the effect and significance of a spread that is increasing or decreasing). The software is going to be constantly scanning the market and then alert you the moment your criteria is met. That kind of assistance is invaluable. You can then watch that go into your terminal, pull up the counter and start looking at what it's doing. You can go from alert to trade in as little as thirty seconds if all the planets are aligned on the deal!

That's just one example. You can flag any number of parameters that you want the software to scan for and have the alert issued when the conditions are met. It is even possible to fine-tune the alerts, and in addition to flagging one condition, you can actually combine a number of conditions. You can say that if X meets this condition, and Y meets that condition and Z meets the other condition — then alert me! This makes a tremendous amount of sense when you are doing cross-crypto arbitrage.

Let's look at an example of how that works. Let's say you have ownership of Bitcoin and that that is your base currency. You set the alert for the scanner to tell you when there is a disparity between BTC, LTC and the USD.

Most pairs work independently of each other so the value relative to each pairing is constantly fluctuating based on the demand and supply of each one's order book. But there are times when you get gaps in the value. For instance let's say that BTC is trading at $10000-70 (remember, this means you buy it at $10,070.00 per BTC and sell it at $10,000.00 per BTC). At the same time, LTC is trading at $220-1.5 (meaning its being bought at $221.5 and sold at $220). But at the same time if you look at the cross rates between BTC and LTC, what you find is a disparity. The reason there should be a balance is this: If you took one of your BTC and sold it in the market, you would get $10,000 for it. If you then took that $10,000 and purchased LTC with it, you should pay $221.50 and that would give you 45.146 LTC. But if the present price of LTC is $230-1.5, that means you can sell 1 LTC and get $230 for it.

This in turn means that selling 45.146 LTC at $230 will get you $10,383.58. So you lock in a $383.58 instant profit because the market is mispriced. This is not an error, it is not illegal and it is not a bad thing to arbitrage your position. In fact you are doing the market a service by keeping the prices correct at all times.

There are just two calculations that go into it. If you are managing six counters to do it at every single variation of price, this will be untenable. But you can definitely have a spreadsheet program running in the background with a life feed and set the alarm to alert you at any point any of the counters experience a mismatch.

If you are going to try to play the arbitrage game, you must be linked into the price mechanism with the lowest latency possible, otherwise you will never be able to even see the window of opportunity, as it will be taken advantage of by somebody else before you are even alerted to the pricing mismatch.

When I first started trading, and was trading exclusively over the internet, I tried in vain many times to execute an arbitrage trade. It never happened because I could never grab the price when it changed. Once I switched to the terminal across a T1 line and optimized the system so that both the data was fast (super low latency) and my spreadsheet was calculating rapidly without other processor sharing apps slowing it down, I found that I could find and pick up an arbitrage opportunity almost once daily.

Finally, you have your price feed which we also talked about. When you get your feed via a terminal like the one we talked about above, then it all integrates nicely and gives you timely information to execute a trade or to liquidate a profit.

This is the kind of speed only a day trader needs. Value traders do not need this kind of speed as they have different ways of negotiating large transactions.

Exchanges

There is one other element which is different from equity markets, and that is the fact that there are multiple exchanges at work, they are all simultaneously operating and they are all open twenty-four hours a day. In an equity market they are mostly exchange hours, and the difference opens you up to better access and higher potential to profit. It also opens up another layer of trading arbitrage.

In the last section we talked about trading arbitrage between cross rates. Having multiple exchanges now allows you to scan real-time prices in different exchanges and cross-trade those when there is a price disparity between two or more exchanges. In an exchange-related arbitrage, what you can do is buy it in one exchange and sell it in other without having to buy a different currency. So let's say you have one exchange quoting BTC at $10,000-70 and another quoting $10,230-00, Then what you can do is instantly lock in two trades where you short the $10,230 and buy the $10,070.00. That would net you a profit of $150 per BTC (this is hypothetical). The occurrence of the exchange disparity is rare — much less than cross-counter disparity. But it is still a potential and you should not leave money on the table by thinking that you will never be able to catch one. Just leave your quote machine and terminal to scan for such an occurrence and you will get the alerts every so often.

Another arbitrage opportunity is for you to be able to get cross rates between currencies across markets. Maybe you purchase BTC in one exchange but trade it in another market because they have a momentary discrepancy in price of LTC per BTC. The reason you do it this way is because markets sometimes lag in price. If you are vigilant, then you get to be the one that corrects the discrepancy and for that you will be rewarded. So you should keep your software looking out for these discrepancies.

There is a fourth avenue for profit that you could exploit in the world of forex and crypto exchanges. That is the forex trading between foreign fiats and bitcoins. This is not something that is widely discussed among the US crypto crowd, but they form a huge piece of the possible profit pie. There is no doubt that the trading between USD and BTC carries the most tradable volume. On a daily basis, it averages approximately $500 million. In a top-ten market, that is about $2 billion. BTC vs. USD indeed is 25% of the trade. However, there are other currencies that you can use to run arbitrage plays all day long. And a person who has a powerful system could run a program to constantly run arbitrage trades like the ones mentioned above and do ones that I will mention here.

There are a couple of pairs that have potential which you should consider, and if you can tune your scanning software and decide to run automated trading software, then it will be possible to take advantage of this arbitrage opportunity.

The first pair you should think about is yen vs. BTC. This is the exchange rate between Japanese yen and Bitcoin. If you want to trade Bitcoin for yen exclusively, that would be a little outside the scope of this book. But the point here is to cross-trade between two fiats and a crypto. In this case you will be doing a dollar/BTC/yen/dollar arbitrage.

It's just as easy as doing the crypto arbitrage with BTC, LTC and the dollar that we looked at earlier. Here is how that would work.

The idea is to san for a price disparity between the three assets — this is assuming you hold the asset in BTC to start with. If you hold it in dollars to start, we'll check out what that would look like in a minute.

This is a hypothetical situation, so let's say the currency quotes are as follows:

USD 10,000-100 per BTC

Yen 110-20 per USD

1,000,000-100 yen per BTC

In this instance, If I enter the market and use 1 BTC to buy $10,000. I then use that USD to buy yen which at 120 yen per dollar would give me 1,200,000 yen. When I instantly convert back to BTC with yen, I get 1.2 BTC.

Sound too good to be true? Well it almost is. That is why cross-currency arbitrage is so well known. With the advent of cryptos, there is a whole new facet to cross-currency arbitrage. In this example you made 1.2 BT — a 20% gain — just because of the market's mispricing. It normally takes less than five minutes to execute the trade and you lock in the profit. Now there are a few provisos. The first is that you need to have a really fast quote and order system. You cannot be late or delay an order, because either someone catches it, or the quotes correct themselves after a couple of trades.

The ability to find disparities gets even more interesting if you add more links in the chain. The key here is the ability to scan in real time and to be able to quickly get the quotes and make the trades.

The second way to profit from this arbitrage is to take it up if you are holding dollars. You can't go in and buy BTC now for the purpose of scalping. Instead you use the $10,000 to purchase 1,100,000 yen. Then you take the Y1,100,000 and purchase BTC. You will get 1.1 BTC. If you convert that back to dollars you will get $11,000. This is a 10% return as opposed to the 20% return earlier. But it is still as close to being free money that you can think of! You of course have to look at the commissions that you will be charged in the three different transactions.

Now that we have a practical path to profiting from the existence of complementary markets and the multitude of exchanges, here is a list of exchanges that you could investigate and read more about. Try to use more than one exchange, especially if you want to conduct cross-exchange arbitrage.

1   Abucoins

2   ACX

3   AEX

4   AidosMarket

5   alcurEX

6   Allcoin

7	Altcoin Trader
8	Bancor Network
9	BarterDEX
10	BCEX
11	Bibox
12	BigONE
13	Binance
14	Bisq
15	Bit-Z
16	Bit2C
17	Bitbank
18	BitBay
19	Bitcoin Indonesia
20	BitcoinToYou
21	BitcoinTrade
22	Bitex
23	Bitfinex
24	BitFlip

25	bitFlyer
26	Bithumb
27	Bitinka
28	BitKonan
29	Bitlish
30	BitMarket
31	Bitmaszyna
32	Bitonic
33	Bits Blockchain
34	Bitsane
35	BitShares Asset Exchange
36	Bitso
37	Bitstamp
38	Bitstamp (Ripple Gateway)
39	Bittrex
40	Bittylicious
41	BL3P
42	Bleutrade

43	Braziliex
44	BTC Markets
45	BTC Trade UA
46	BTC-Alpha
47	BTCC
48	BtcTrade
49	BTCTurk
50	Burst Asset Exchange
51	BX Thailand
52	C-CEX
53	C-Patex
54	C2CX
55	CEX
56	ChaoEX
57	Cobinhood
58	Coinbe
59	Coinbene
60	CoinCorner

61 CoinEgg
62 CoinEx
63 CoinExchange
64 CoinFalcon
65 Coinfloor
66 Coingi
67 Coinhouse
68 Coinlink
69 CoinMate
70 Coinnest
71 Coinone
72 Coinrail
73 Coinrate
74 Coinroom
75 CoinsBank
76 Coinsecure
77 Coinsquare
78 Coinut

79	COSS
80	Counterparty DEX
81	CryptoBridge
82	CryptoDerivatives
83	CryptoMarket
84	Cryptomate
85	Cryptopia
86	Cryptox
87	DC-Ex
88	DDEX
89	Dgtmarket
90	DSX
91	ETHEXIndia
92	ExcambrioRex
93	Exchange
94	Exmo
95	Exrates
96	EXX

97	ezBtc
98	Fargobase
99	Fatbtc
100	Foxbit
101	FreiExchange
102	Gate
103	Gatecoin
104	Gatehub
105	GDAX
106	Gemini
107	GetBTC
108	GuldenTrader
109	Heat Wallet
110	HitBTC
111	Huobi
112	IDAX
113	IDEX
114	Independent Reserve

115	InfinityCoin Exchange
116	Iquant
117	ISX
118	itBit
119	Koineks
120	Koinex
121	Koinim
122	Korbit
123	Kraken
124	Kucoin
125	Kuna
126	LakeBTC
127	Lbank
128	LEOxChange
129	Liqui
130	LiteBit
131	Livecoin
132	LocalTrade

133	Luno
134	Lykke Exchange
135	Mercado Bitcoin
136	Mercatox
137	Mr
138	Negocie Coins
139	Neraex
140	NIX-E
141	Nocks
142	OasisDEX
143	OEX
144	OKCoin
145	OkCoin Intl
146	OKEx
147	Omni DEX
148	OpenLedger DEX
149	Ore
150	Paribu

151 Paymium

152 Poloniex

153 QBTC

154 Qryptos

155 QuadrigaCX

156 Quoine

157 Radar Relay

158 Rfinex

159 RightBTC

160 Rippex

161 Ripple China

162 RippleFox

163 Simex

164 SouthXchange

165 Stellar Decentralized Exchange

166 Stronghold

167 SurBTC

168 TCC Exchange

169	TDAX
170	The Rock Trading
171	Tidebit
172	Tidex
173	Token Store
174	TOPBTC
175	Trade By Trade
176	Trade Satoshi
177	TradeOgre
178	Tripe Dice Exchange
179	Tux Exchange
180	Upbit
181	Vebitcoin
182	VirtacoinWorld
183	Waves Decentralized Exchange
184	WEX
185	xBTCe
186	YoBit

187   Zaif

188   ZB

189   Zebpay

** Note: These are sites that have not been vetted. You need to do your own due diligence before using their services.

Trading Strategies

For those of you who already know the basics, you could have skipped the first two chapters and headed straight here, because this is where the nuts and bolts are. After you have done your homework and you have read the fundamentals, the keys to operational strategies and trading routines are contained within this chapter.

Trading strategies come in the layer after the understanding of the fundamentals of the company and the understanding of the market in general. In all trades, your frame of mind is structured in four layers. The deepest layer is the understanding of the underlying micro and macro economy. If the underlying economy is overwhelmingly bullish, then you know that there is always going to be an upward bias in the overall condition of the stock market.

The second thing is that you are going to understand

the sector which you are trading in. If you are looking at Apple, then you are going to look at the electronics sector and understand the bias in that sector, and if it is an upswing or a retracement. This is built on top of your position on the first layer of the economy.

The third thing is the company itself and their earnings, their fundamentals and their advances. This is company-specific and you have to have an opinion and understanding of the company itself.

Finally, it's about the characteristic of the market which is a culmination and effect of the rules of the market, the culture of the market and the manner in which it behaves. For instance, stocks on an open outcry market will tend to have different trading characteristics than a market that uses software to match prices. These are the kinds of things you need to learn from reading and from actually doing and getting the experience you need.

These four areas are important if you really want to be a long-term day trader and it is something that you have to keep your mind open to while responding to the changes and developments on a daily basis.

By the way, this is an ongoing thing. Even when you are on vacation, you may not be making actual trades, but you should keep up with the market and keep tabs on the counters that you usually trade.

The first thing you are going to do is adjust your head.

By that I mean you need to have a certain mindset to be able to take this market by its horns and move it to your will. It is entirely doable but you need to do this smartly. You can't rush into things. If you miss this opportunity, there will be another one; never chase a trade or force an opportunity.

You will make mistakes — know that as factually as you know the sun rises in the morning. But just because you know you are going to make mistakes does not mean that you don't play the market. Day trading was the biggest tool I used to learn about myself. It is amazing how much about yourself you do not know, and once you start to make mistakes in the market you learn so quickly.

For a day trader, fluctuations are the best thing in the world. You have to know that and you have to believe that. Why are fluctuations your best friend? Because when a market fluctuates you have the opportunity to make money each time it rises and each time it falls. A long-term trader looks at a market and sees that the price is stable in a band between $20 and $25 and he says that the stock is trading in a band and that there is nothing he can do to make money. Wrong!

When the market is in a trading band there are two things you want to do. First you want to make a determination why it's in a trading range. The second thing you want is to get a handle on which side it's going to break. The third thing you want to know is what the volume of transaction is on any given day.

When you know this, you set to work. A band is one of the best ways to make money for a day trader because you know very clearly where your upper trading limit is, and where your lower trading limit is. So what you do is enter an order at the bottom band — go in long, obviously. Then at a mark, fifteen percent below the band top, you execute a sell. But there are two kinds of sell that you can do here. The first type of sell is to liquidate the earlier buy order. The second sell is to create a new short.

There are two ways you can do this.

The first way is to enter both orders at the same time. When you buy at $1 and sell at $1.9, here is what that looks like when you make the trade. Buying in at $1 means that the spread was approximately $0.90-00. That means when you went long, the sell price was $0.90 and the buy price was $1.00. When the market went to $1.90 on the sell, the buy was sitting at $2.00. So when you execute the flip, you liquidate your $1 position at $1.90 and you short your position at $1.90 as well. You must understand that at this point right away, you are in the hole for a dime. But if the band is right, then the price is going to start coming back down and it will return to $0.90-00. When it gets to that point, place a buy for the short sell you made earlier and place another buy for a new position in anticipation of it climbing back up.

The second way you can do this is to be a little more conservative. This is the way you should do it if you are just starting out and you want to use this to test the theories and get used to the market's pulse.

If you do the same thing with the stock and buy in at $1.00 when the price is $0.90-00, then you will wait till it gets to the sell point at $1.90-00. You would sell at $1.90 to liquidate and wait until the market continues on its own steam. When it reaches its apex and starts its retreat, you mark it at 5% of its peak and get back in again and that should be about $1.90 (on its way down as opposed to on its way up in the last scenario). You keep doing this by staggering the two sell or the two buy orders when you need to make them.

In the first instance, the point where it reaches your price point is the point for the first liquidation. Then you wait until it reaches its peak. The moment it reaches its peak and indicates a reversal, you enter the short order at the same price point or thereabouts (take the 5% rule) and ride the market on the way down again. When it reaches the 5% mark short of the bottom point, you liquidate the short and wait for the reversal to get back up and enter again.

Go to your historical price chart and look for a stock that has bands, then look at the hourly or minute-by-minute historical and see how many times it bounces back and forth. These are all the times a swing or position trader would completely avoid and miss the opportunity.

Warren Buffett said that you should never be afraid of fluctuations. Of course he didn't mean it in terms of day trading, but his advice nonetheless still holds true.

When you trade the rise and fall of any stock, then what you are doing is optimizing the movement of the market. There are so many counters that move sideways and those are the counters you want to attack with all the ferocity of a shark!

As a day trader, fluctuation is your best friend. You don't need to tame it and you don't need to fear it. You need to ride it. You hardly find value traders or swing traders taking advantage of these price movements, and you should.

Let's be clear about one more thing here. When you scalp these markets or day trade, actually the day trading strategy and the scalping strategy are almost the same. I am not really sure why people have the desire to try and redefine the two. You are day trading. And if you are not entering the market and riding the momentum or riding the momentary sentiment, then you are not day trading. You need an almost psychic touch to maneuver this market under this

Day trading is about picking up every penny that you can and doing it within the parameters of spreads and fluctuations. The most predictable of the price movements are in the range trading, but by no means is that the only time you want to enter the market. If you are only looking for range trading, then you are going to miss out on about 98% of the other kinds of moments that traders look for.

Retracements

Here is another kind of market movement that you have to look out for. This one is both counter specific and market specific. In a stable market, where the moving forces are not macro in nature, what you will find is that the counter needs to breathe. This means that whichever way it is riding, it has to retrace its steps before mounting another charge.

As a day trader, you want to make money on all the dimensions of a price movement. That means you want to make money going up, going down, going sideways and when it is retracing.

The logic then is that you want some kind of insight into the subsequent move of the market.

It turns out that markets do indeed move in predictable steps — just not predictable to the casual watcher. But they do move predictably in relation to market forces, and that brings us to the realm of probability and statistics.

Everything is connected by statistics and probability if you know how to appreciate it. If I throw a coin in the air, it will land on one of two sides — right? Sure, we know this. The key is to know which side. If you throw it exactly the same way, over a million times you will find that the incidence of heads to the incidence of tales will approach 50%. If nothing else, you need to look at statistics in this stable understanding. That means that nature is equally balanced. But remember — as I've mentioned already — the price of a stock is not based on chance. The price of a stock is also not based on probability. But its fluctuations are, and as a day trader, that is what you are going after.

So if you set aside macro plays, corporate plays and sector plays, and you already understand the grand scheme of those movements, what you are left to decipher, at the granular level of fluctuations, is not about macro factors anymore. It is about the momentum of the market manifesting itself in the movements of price. That can be calculated and predicted, but still not accurately 100% of the time. Because it is not 100%, what you must do is put in place a stopgap measure and backstops to prevent the error of a position going forward unchecked.

For this reason you have stop orders, market orders and limit orders so that you do not unintentionally careen past your price points.

Let me be clear about this. You still need to understand

the macro play that happens at the fundamental level (i.e., economics, corporate finance and sentiment), but then you also have to predict the market movements via charts and strategies. That brings you to the major part of this chapter and this book concerning using charting methods and technical analysis to understand what the market is doing and what it is about to do.

The first and the simplest one that we are going to look at is the ADX indicator. But before we get to that, we need to make sure you get some moving average superimposed on tot the price chart. This will help give you trend and behavior.

Moving Average

The moving average can be calculated for almost any number of periods or any number of sensitivities. In many cases you see the moving average of the closing price over the last three days. It's moving because the last number drops off and is replaced by the current number. So, it works like this for a three-day moving average:

Take the most recent closing price, add that to the closing price of the day prior, and add that to the closing price of the day before that one. So if you are now at the close of January 10th, you add January

10th's closing price to the closing price from the 9th plus the closing from the 8th. Then you divide by the number of days you are doing — in this case, that's three.

So let's suppose your stock closed at $10 on the 10th, $9 on the 9th and $8 on the 8th. Then you add 10+9+8 which equals 27, then divide that by 3 to give you the three-day moving average, which for today is $9. You can use this for any number of period classes. So for instance, I could have a twenty-one-day moving average and just add up all the closing prices for the last twenty-one days and divide them by 21. That would give me the average for today. And when tomorrow ended I would do the same, in effect adding tomorrow's close to the group but dropping off the close from the furthest date.

This is a standard way to see the tides of the market and you should use this to see the overall trend. A good number to pick is 13 periods. You can use two forms of periods. You can either use the daily periods or you can use the minute periods. If you see the minute periods that means that you will see the trends of the last thirteen minutes and it will give you a good basic trend representation. But this is not your primary indicator or trade entry signal generator. You need tools that are more sophisticated than that.

I typically use 13 and 21 periods on the minute chart, 8 and 13 periods on a daily chart and 89 and 55 days on a yearly chart. The reason you use two lines is because they are of varying sensitivities. A cross over indicates a change in trend in the long, mid and short term.

Exponential Moving Average

Just like the Moving Average (MA) you saw above, the EMA also looks at the average of a trailing number of data points. Except the difference is that it pays more weight to the number that is more in the recent past than the one that is further past. So let's say you have 10 from three days ago, 8 from two days ago and 6 from today. More weight is given to the 6, and the least weight given to 10. So if the MA for those three numbers is 9 ((10+9+8)/3) then the EMA would be calculated as follows (for example): 10(0.6)+9(0.3)+8(0.1) = 9.5. So the difference is that the MA gives all three prices equal weight while the EMA gives the most recent price more weight. How much weight you want to give each number is up to you and should be based on mathematical reasoning and tempered with experience.

The EMA is popular because it is the basis of a number of other signaling tools including the ADX indicator that we will talk about below, and the MACD (Moving Average Convergence-Divergence) indicator.

The advantage that the EMA has to regular MA is that it is more relevant to the present than the latter. Here is why. Day traders need signals that trigger as close to entry and exit points. MA is a slow-changing laggard in which the trigger of crossing over only happens after the optimal entry or exit happens. If you only follow the MA, then you will always enter the market late and exit the market late. This opens you up to the risk of diminished profits and the possibility of loss as well. So following MA to enter and exit is not a good idea. This is where EMA comes into play.

Average True Range

The ATR is a simple measure that analyzes a stock and quantifies its volatility by looking at the range from the close of the previous session to the high of the current session. It is take in terms of absolute value so even the direction is negative, the value that is desired will be the absolute value of the quantum. The reason this is so is because the number that is needed is not designed to indicate direction, only to indicate quantum. TR looks at the travel for the close of the last to the high of the present. If that present is higher it results in a naturally positive number, and if the high is lower than the close, it is a natural negative number that is made absolute by definition.

Once you have the true range of the period, then you can calculate the average of the last number of periods. You can fiddle with this to get one that works for your counter. I typically use 13 and 21.

Date

Open

High

Low

Close

Volume

MA3

MA5

MA8

TR

ATR

02/02/2018

166

166.8

160.1

160.5

85,957,050

165.2366667

166.128

168.435

0.98

1.232978571

02/01/2018

167.165

168.62

166.76

167.78

44,453,230

167.3933333

168.33

170.5025

1.19

1.31155

01/31/2018

166.87

168.4417

166.5

167.43

32,234,520

167.4533333

168.996

171.655

1.4717

1.312164286

01/30/2018

165.525

167.37

164.7

166.97

45,635,470

168.8133333

170.354

173.03375

0.59

1.209185714

01/29/2018

170.16

170.16

167.07

167.96

50,565,420

170.1933333

172.368

174.57

1.35

1.217757143

01/26/2018

172

172

170.06

171.51

39,075,250

172.28

174.176

175.9625

0.89

1.1649

01/25/2018

174.505

174.95

170.53

171.11

41,438,280

174.1233333

175.566

176.5475

0.73

1.268471429

01/24/2018

177.25

177.3

173.2

174.22

51,368,540

176.0866667

177.196

177.295

0.26

1.3049

01/23/2018

177.3

179.44

176.82

177.04

32,395,870

177.5

178.172

177.4275

2.44

1.4499

01/22/2018

177.3

177.78

176.6016

177

27,052,000

178.24

178.002

177.08375

0.68

01/19/2018

178.61

179.58

177.41

178.46

31,306,390

178.94

178.02

176.75

0.32

01/18/2018

179.37

180.1

178.25

179.26

31,087,330

178.1833333

177.384

176.23625

1

01/17/2018

176.15

179.25

175.07

179.1

34,260,230

177.46

176.39

175.70375

3.06

01/16/2018

177.9

179.39

176.14

176.19

29,512,410

176.1866667

175.436

174.945

2.3

01/12/2018

176.18

177.36

175.65

177.09

25,302,200

175.5533333

175.068

174.45

2.08

01/11/2018

174.59

175.4886

174.49

175.28

18,653,380

174.6333333

174.65

1.1986

01/10/2018

173.16

174.3

173

174.29

23,751,690

174.3233333

174.2

0.03

01/09/2018

174.55

175.06

173.41

174.33

21,532,200

174.56

173.788

0.71

01/08/2018

174.35

175.61

173.93

174.35

20,523,870

174.1266667

0.61

01/05/2018

173.44

175.37

173.05

175

23,589,930

173.42

2.34

01/04/2018

172.54

173.47

172.08

173.03

22,342,650

172.5066667

1.24

01/03/2018

172.53

174.55

171.96

172.23

29,461,040

2.29

01/02/2018

170.16

172.3

169.26

172.26

25,400,540

172.3

So this is what that would look like. If you look at the APPL counter numbers above, you will see what the ATR should look like. The ATR in this example is calculated at 14 days.

ADX Indicator

The ADX Indicator is the one that helps us with a slightly larger view of the market. It gives us an underlying bias and tells us what direction the market is going to break when it does. Let me first tell you the reasoning behind it and then tell you how to read it. The underlying issue behind it is the fact that it is identifying trends in price and thus the reversal of trends. This is a long-term tool and you should look at this for technical direction. Let's say that the tool has signified a change in trend — perhaps from an upward trend, to a change, and on to a downward trend. This kind of move should be something that you see as a guideline to say that even if you enter the make it in a narrow band, you know that your risk is always on the short side. Because you know that the overall trend is to break lower.

This is an important indicator to have. It determines how you treat your entry and exit. If you are in an upward trend, then you can ride the upswings further and cut your downswings shorter. Why? Because remember there are retracements in every market as a day trader, it makes sense to catch as many traders as you can, and to do that, you want to catch a trade on its upswing and on its retracement down. So when the ADX swings to a buy, then your buys are kept longer and your sells are kept shorter. When the ADX shows a declining market then your shorts are help longer and your longs are held for lesser time.

Here is how ADX works.

It is plotted below the actual price chart, in corresponding columns. So for instance, if your price chart is using minute-by-minute candlesticks that show open, high, low and close prices, then directly beneath that candlestick in the chart below, you will din a point for the value on the ADX. The ADX is really a line chart and plots one point for each candlesticks.

The ADX goes between 0 (the lowest it can go to) and 100 (the highest it can reach), regardless of how high the market ascends or descends. That is because the ADX line does not show your piece; it shows your relative strength. It is also called a momentum indicator because it can quantify the momentum of a counter, but it is also used as a directional strength if you use it properly.

The way it is calculated if you are using a minute-by-minute candlestick chart, is to track the change from the last period's high to this period's high — so the most current point will constantly be flipping while the bar is still in the active period. You then take the current high and subtract the last period's high. This will give you a positive or a negative number (whether positive or negative is important). If it is a negative number, then you take it as "zero." If it is a positive number, then you keep that positive number. If this period's high is higher than the last period, you are going to get a positive number. If the current high is lower than the last high, you are going to get a negative number, so you will then notate zero.

Then you take the previous low and subtract the present low from that. Note that the order is reversed.

In the high, you use the current high and subtract the previous high from it. In the low, you take the previous low and subtract the current low from it. If you get a positive number, use that. If you get a negative number, than you notate zero.

Once you have the two numbers, you need to compare them. You can then go on to process them with the other averages. Don't worry; you do not need to do this by hand. It depends on the data service that you use. The premium ones will already have them within the package, but the less expensive ones might not. So just in case you don't have those, here is how you program the spreadsheet to calculate this for yourself.

You already know how to get the +DM and the -DM. Now you need to get the Average True Range. The ATR is a measure of volatility that is measured specifically so that you can include them in your calculations for things like the ADX. We showed you how to calculate them above.

Here are the steps you need to go through to get the rest of the way and plot the ADX:

Once you have the TR, PDM and MDM, smooth them using an appropriate number of days. They can all be the same number. So if you use 8 periods to smooth the TR, then use eight days to smooth the PDM and the MDM as well. In the above example I used 14.

Next, divide the smooth PDM by the smoothed TR.

This will give you the Directional Indicator - abbreviated as 8PDI (it's 8 because I used 8 periods in the calculation; change the number to the number of periods you use) and then multiply this by 100.

Do the same with the MDM. Now take the MDM and divide it by the TR. This will give you the 8MDI. Then multiply that by 100.

Now subtract the 8MDI from the 8PDI (use the absolute value of the subtraction) then divide that by the sum of the two numbers — |(8PDI-8MDI)|/(8PDI+8MDI) then multiply this by 100. This is your Directional Index. You still have one more step to go.

You should be able to get the Directional Index for each period, now all you have to do is get the average, so take the DI for the last 13 periods and add them up, then divide them by 13. That will give you the ADX.

Now that you have the ADX, what do you do with it?

The ADX is a smooth indicator for buy and sell signals. Its sensitivity varies with the periods you use. If you use hours, you get a less sensitive metric as opposed to using it with minutes. If you use days, it is less sensitive than hours. For day trading, it is best to use it with minute-by-minute candlestick charts for the best indications.

For indications of ADX between 0 and 25, that

indicates that there ideally isn't any trend in this time range. That's not a bad thing if the time periods you used were hourly. Add on and do one more for the minute-by-minute, and you will see that the ADX changes. What this may tell you is that while there is no trend in the hourly charts, there may be a trend in the minute charts.

Between 25 and 50 indicates a strong trend and you should be on the alert to make a move. Between 50 and 75 shows a very strong trend and you should enter the market in the direction you see the chart moving. Once it goes into the 75-100 range, you'll find it to be the highest certainty of a trend.

Trading Gaps at the Open

There is a rule of thumb that has yet to be proven wrong in all my days as a trader. The rule is fairly simple but must be corroborated with other signals. This rule of thumb predicts that anytime there is a gap, especially at the opening and no matter how far the market peels away, it will retrace itself to close the gap before getting back on its way.

To understand the nature of the gap, you have to look at the price after the gap occurs. The kind of gap that it turns out to be is dependent on the way the price behaves after the event.

There are four kinds of gaps and there are consequently eight gap trading strategies that you should be aware of. We will start by identifying the kinds of gaps there are and then take it from there.

The first is called a Full Gap Up. So let's say you have a stock that closed at $10 with a high of $12, and it opened at $14 and went up. You can expect that the market will retrace back to a point close to that gap between $14 and $12. The gap is not between the close and the open but the high and the open

The second is called a Full Gap Down and it is exactly the same as the first one, except the direction is opposite. A full gap down occurs when the open is below yesterday's lowest price. So if the price closed at $10 and the previous low was $8, and the counter opened at $6, that would constitute a gap.

The third kind of gap is when the current open is above the previous close but not above the previous high. So let's say the highest yesterday was $14 and closed at $10, then today it opened at $12. Because it opened higher than the close but lower than the high, it is a partial gap up.

The fourth and final kind is when the gap is a partial gap down. This is when the price opens lower than the previous day's close but higher than the previous low.

Now that we get an understanding of the lay of the land as far as gaps go, now let's look at the rationale and the strategies to take advantage of them on the open.

The point that I have to mention here is that this is not meant to be used in in day trading. That means if you are following a candlestick chart that is on a minute-by-minute scale, and it goes from one period to the next with a gap up or one of the other gaps, this strategy doesn't work. It is purely for trading gaps at the open of the day.

Now that we know the kinds of trading gaps there are, let's look at the mechanics of what is going on. Each gap gives you the potential for two kinds of trades. You can do either a long or a short. That's why you have eight possible strategies for four possible gaps.

Your first strategy is to enter two trades at the market open — one for a long position and the other for a short. Ideally use the same lot size so if you are buying ten lots, make sure you short ten lots. Also be sure that you are doing two separate orders, because that way they don't cancel each other out.

The reason you do this is because there are price potentials in both directions and you want to be able to catch both. If this is a gap up then your long order has a 10% trailing stop. This means that when the price climbs, there is a liquidation order that follows it. This is what it would look like. If the market opens at $10 (with yesterday's high let's say at $7) place a buy at market and place a sell at market. For the buy order, place a Trailing Stop Limit Sell. This will make sure that as the market climbs, so will the trigger to liquidate the position. Set the trailing stop at 8% of the market price. The trailing price only follows as long as the price increases. The moment the price traces back, it stops at the 8% level of the last highest level the price reached. So if you were at $10 when the market started to retrace, the trigger would be at $9.20 ($2.2 above your original buy position).

Chapter 5

Future of Bitcoin

There is a tremendous amount of anxiety with the future of bitcoin and the future of cryptocurrency in general. There are three things that you need to know about how the world of cryptocurrency is going to unfold.

The first is that there is no sovereign system of laws that can effectively block the use of bitcoin or diminish the existence of a blockchain. To outlaw it is one thing, and could be attempted, but to enforce it is quite another. One thing for sure, though, is that old-economy institutions will not stop trying to put a halt to specific currencies, but at the same time they can't deny the efficacy of the blockchain.

The second is that there are numerous bad actors who have had greater foresight than the learned economists, and the net effect has resulted in the cryptocurrency scene being dominated by news of ill use of the technology. Do not be fooled by the fact that all of bitcoin is tainted. So are fiats. Researchers in the UK studied this issue and were able to tag bitcoins that were used for illegal activities, and the most they could find out was that about 13% of bitcoins had been stolen and/or used for illicit activity. I suspect that is significantly less than the percentage of illegal activity conducted using fiats.

Finally, the creation, adoption and use of bitcoins and all cryptocurrencies has been organic and against the odds. The technology is sound and the concept is compelling. As the world grows closer and international trade increases, with or without the United States, bitcoin and the rest of the cryptos will continue to be a viable and superior option for value transfer.

That being said, and as optimistic as the majority of tech-savvy users are globally, there is always a risk. And you need to always do a reality check and understand what you are getting in to. If you are getting into it for mining and making an income from it, then your considerations may be a little different from someone who is doing it purely to remain off the grid and using it to be untraceable. That sort of usage is not as prevalent as you may think, although it is a strong added feature. Either way, do not shortchange the need for privacy. In the age of Big Data, the use of online shopping creates tremendously accurate psychological profiles that can be used against you.

The use and the depth of Bitcoin will only get stronger and deeper over time. The technology will improve and the adoption rate will increase especially as we move to the Internet of Things and advance into mobile computing. New technologies, built on Bitcoin will unfold and improvements to the blockchain will be developed.

It is impossible to stop something whose time has come.

Conclusion

The future of Bitcoin is fairly robust. There are old-school economists who look at Bitcoin and the Blockchain that it sits on with contempt, and they are right to a certain extent. Bitcoin is not ready to take over the world's transactions. For one thing, there are only 21 million coins and then there are 100 million Satoshis per coin, making 2.1 Billion Satoshis in all. That would not be enough to cover the world's transactions,. It can't even cover the transactions in the US which amount to 19 trillion dollars. The thinking that Bitcoin could become a major currency is not lucid.

However, Bitcoin has its place in the online world and it's not only illegal activities that are claimed to rely on Bitcoin. That's another fallacy you shouldn't pay heed to. Privacy is an important part of a world that is trying to know so many things about you and your patterns, and Bitcoin certainly provides that – to the dismay of the corporate world and government bodies. Think about this whole Facebook/Cambridge Analytica issue about trying to get into your head. If they don't know you, they can't get into your head. Bitcoin goes a long way in making sure that your patterns are shielded from prying eyes.

It tickles me to hear people say that if you have nothing

to hide, why do you need privacy? That's not the point. Millions of people had nothing to hide and let their information hang out, while large data companies parsed them and used them to target their messages – commercial and political. Bitcoin and the Blockchain can change that.

It removes the issue of trust and the institutions that were built to guarantee trust. And those institutions are going to fight tooth and nail to see that they are not displaced by something like Blockchains and distributed technologies.

Are there problems with Bitcoin? Yes, of course there are. This is still the first iteration of a cryptocurrency that works. We have a long way to go yet and many more iterations to contemplate and mistakes to make. Bitcoin is still resource-heavy due to its proof of work. It takes up millions of dollars in electricity costs. That would not be so bad once the grid is predominantly driven by green energy, but right now it's not, and so there is a carbon footprint that does have many concerned. It may be sufficient for a small issue like Bitcoin, but it will not be something that will sustain a global currency. In light of this, there are other blockchain proofs that are being brought online – like Proof Stake and others.

Bitcoin stands at the leading edge of a seismic shift in the way society interacts, exchanges value, transmits information and relates to each other. There's a tremendous amount of opportunity available from mining it to trading it, and developing applications and systems using it. How you use it once you have the benefit of the knowledge in this book is up to you, but remember that Bitcoin and the Blockchain are here to stay.

Thank You!

Before you go, we would like to thank you for purchasing a copy of our book. Out of the dozens of books you could have picked over ours, you decided to go with this one and for that we are very grateful.

We hope you enjoyed reading it as much as we enjoyed writing it! We hope you found it very informative.

We would like to ask you for a small favor. Could you please take a moment to leave a review for this book on Amazon?

Your feedback will help us continue to write more books and release new content in the future!

Don't Forget to Download Your Bonus:

Bitcoin Profit Secrets

https://dibblypublishing.com/bitcoin-profit-secrets

More Books by

Crypto Tech Academy

- Cryptocurrency Trading: A Complete Beginners Guide to Cryptocurrency Investing with Bitcoin, Litecoin, Ethereum, Altcoin, Ripple, Dogecoin, Dash, and Others
- Cryptocurrency Mining: A Complete Beginners Guide to Mining Cryptocurrencies, Including Bitcoin, Litecoin, Ethereum, Altcoin, Monero, and Others
- Blockchain: A Complete Beginners Guide to the Technology Powering Bitcoin & Cryptocurrencies

www.ingramcontent.com/pod-product-compliance
Lightning Source LLC
Chambersburg PA
CBHW020427220526
45464CB00002B/595